Praise for

HIGH FLIGHT

"Richard's unforgettable, inspirational journey is one of grit, courage, survival, resilience, and love. His is a uniquely American story, and he is a true American hero."

—Doug Williams, author of *Failure Point*, playwright, award-winning screenwriter, and filmmaker

"Just another book written by a pilot, right? Not at all! This book was written by a man with a real zest for life, who just so happens to be a pilot. Richard has flown just about everything with wings: high-performance combat aircraft, relics from bygone eras, as well as Boeing wide-bodies. Climb aboard, strap in, and fly with Rick as he takes you through an amazing career that spans more than fifty years and logs over 28,000 hours."

—MSgt Johnny Gressett, USAF (Ret), author of *Tumbletite*

"Richard Hess's memoir demonstrates that a person's journey through life does not follow a straight or predictable path. It is obvious that the trials and tribulations of family life, accompanied by warm and loving relationships, forged a man of strength and determination, but also a person with a sense of compassion.

Richard's passion for all facets of aviation is the glue that binds his stories of travel and adventure together. His devotion to his family and global friendships makes this man's saga a compelling read, and his many accomplishments illustrate that there is always a new challenge in life. After each accomplishment, he asks himself the question, 'What will I do next?'"

—Jack Bartley, US Navy (Ret), author of *Smoke on the Water*

"Somewhere in Richard Hess's memoir are the words "Thank goodness for the US Air Force." I can't think of a better way to sum up or recommend this book. After being burdened with his abusive stepfather's name, the Air Force saved the author from an unhappy upbringing and offered him a career, camaraderie, leadership, and respect. But none of that would have happened without his drive, his innate talent for aviation, or his capacity for hard work.

The guy's life is a whirlwind: Thirteen years of active military duty, followed by fifteen years in the Air National Guard (with several deployments to the Middle East), overlapping with thirty-one years flying for the airlines, where he captained Boeing 777 passenger jets, topped off with decades of ever-shifting and challenging business ventures. And there's no airframe, it seems, he hasn't flown. Richard has a photographic memory as he recreates many of the biggest and smallest incidents in his life. This book is perfect for aviation geeks, but the most enticing passages of *High Flight* occur when he writes about his feelings for his family. His captivating story is one you'll devour from the first page to the last."

—Richard Scott Sacks, author of *Drinking from the Stream*

"A difficult childhood is often used as an excuse by those who fail in life. The opposite is the case for Richard Hess. His harsh youth forged his faith, determination, and character. His story describes his journey from deprivation to a glowing, multifaceted career as a savvy USAF officer and combat pilot, a senior captain at Delta Air Lines, a successful business owner, and, more recently, a gifted author. *High Flight: A Pilot's Journey Through Life* is an inspiring all-American success story that will leave every reader a better person."

—Robert Lutz, former Marine Corps fighter pilot and retired vice-chairman of General Motors

"In his memoir, Richard Hess describes growing up with fewer resources than what many children have nowadays. His hardships in childhood served him well in the military. As an officer in the Air Force, he was expected to grow into managerial roles, and he was activated in a leadership position for ten months in the first Desert Storm. His story begins with a heartrending home situation but ends with brilliancy and optimism. *High Flight* is a must-read valentine to life. I highly recommend it."

—Tony Dora, author of *A Boy, an Orphanage, a Cuban Refugee: The Road to Freedom*

High Flight
A Pilot's Journey Through Life
by Richard Hess

© Copyright 2025 Richard Hess

ISBN 979-8-88824-715-0

All rights reserved. No part of this publication may be reproduced, stored in a retrieval system, or transmitted in any form or by any means—electronic, mechanical, photocopy, recording, or any other—except for brief quotations in printed reviews, without the prior written permission of the author.

Published by

◤ köehlerbooks™

3705 Shore Drive
Virginia Beach, VA 23455
800-435-4811
www.koehlerbooks.com

HIGH FLIGHT

A Pilot's Journey Through Life

RICHARD HESS

VIRGINIA BEACH
CAPE CHARLES

This book is dedicated to my loving wife of fifty years, Rosann. Who else could have tolerated my absences while I was gallivanting the globe for half a century? Because of you, and the family we have raised, my life has meaning. I love you.

Foreword

Rich likes to tell the story, usually with a smirky grin, of the day he saved my life. He saved not only mine, but his own and our entire C-141 crew when a wayward Cessna suddenly appeared in our windscreen. With no time to talk he disconnected the autopilot and maneuvered the Starlifter away from the Cessna's path.

He proclaims I reciprocated by saving *his* life, but in a different way. I introduced him to the captivating world of sport and warbird flying, and he pursued it with the resolve of a fighter pilot closing for a gun kill. He rapidly became a sought-after instructor in L-39 jets and other splendid flying machines of the Soviet era that made their way into Western hands after the Iron Curtain fell. That led to his establishment of a foreign-jet overhaul and maintenance service that spread into Europe and Africa. He became a premier oceanic ferry pilot making numerous solo crossings in single-engine jets over the treacherous North Atlantic. When he was not doing this really fun stuff, he pushed Delta's Boeing 777s around the sky. Even after hanging up his Delta spurs, he wasn't done. He started yet another career flying corporate jets. His unrelenting kinetic energy confounded me, but I discovered he also had plenty of potential energy.

Knowing he loved to write and had published several magazine stories about his experiences in the warbird community, I invited him to join with me in writing a military-aviation thriller, *Night of the Bear*, involving those Communist warbirds that we learned so much about, and even owned and flew. His creative-writing learning curve astounded me, and I knew he would make a name for himself in the community of authors.

A plethora of retiring pilots are eager to tell their stories, and Rich is certainly one of them. But many of those biographies are heavy on hairy tales of derring-do and light on transparency in their personal lives. With *High Flight: A Pilot's Journey Through Life*, Rich has shown us his feelings, his failings, and his mistakes—the same things we pilots all possess but are reluctant to talk about. Humility is not in our DNA, but life in the air issues us an attention-getting ration of it now and then. We're loath to admit it. So is Rich, but he doesn't hold anything back.

Rich's life story balances and contrasts the thrill and excitement of flight with his early struggles in a dismally dysfunctional family. With such an upbringing, many young people would have bailed out on achieving a productive life and gone the way of addiction and turpitude. Not Rich. Guided by his faith in God, he chose the path of perseverance, hard work, and success. You'll enjoy riding with him in peace and war, in the cockpits of T-38s, A-10s, F-15s, C-141s, and a wide variety of civil aircraft. Best of all, you'll see the boy, and eventually the man, who endured heartbreak, hardship, challenge, and danger to achieve his dream of reaching the pinnacle of aviation.

—Captain Alan Cockrell, United Airlines (Ret.), author of *Tail of the Storm* and coauthor of *Night of the Bear*

HIGH FLIGHT
By John Gillespie Magee Jr.

Oh! I have slipped the surly bonds of Earth
And danced the skies on laughter-silvered wings;
Sunward I've climbed, and joined the tumbling mirth
of sun-split clouds,—and done a hundred things
You have not dreamed of—wheeled and soared and swung
High in the sunlit silence. Hov'ring there,
I've chased the shouting wind along, and flung
My eager craft through footless halls of air . . .

Up, up the long, delirious, burning blue
I've topped the wind-swept heights with easy grace
Where never lark, or even eagle flew—
And, while with silent lifting mind I've trod
The high untrespassed sanctity of space,
Put out my hand, and touched the face of God.

CHAPTER 1

Till Death Do Us Part

My daughter Diana, a Colorado college student at the time, called me late one night. Seems she had traveled to Connecticut to see my father, John, that week. He was seventy-four and dying of cancer. It started in his liver and spread to his lungs. The doctors didn't expect him to live out the month. The painful coincidence is that we had just buried my mother not fifteen months before. She was a lifelong smoker and died at seventy, her body riddled with cancer.

I no longer had a relationship with my father, but after the initial pain of the family's split, I was thankful my children did. However, what Diana had to say was quite upsetting. Her aunt Ann, my half-sister, had asked her to have me call her.

Diana said, "She wants to have a relationship with you."

My response was, "So let her call me." My relationship with my half-brother, Jeff, and my half-sister, Ann, was severely strained due to their mother, Viola, as I'll explain. I was hurt from being shunned by the very people I wanted to be close to.

A relationship, no matter which two people make it up, is much like a marriage. Each person brings certain strengths and weaknesses to the table. Usually, in a good relationship, each makes up for the other's weakness—that is, where you're weak, I'm strong, and where I'm weak, you're strong. Also, like a marriage, sometimes the relationship sours. The reasons are as numerous as blades of grass.

However, once one party or the other no longer wishes to continue the bond, gaining back the synergy, peace, or harmony of the "marriage" is nearly impossible.

Our feelings are like the clothing we carry in a suitcase. As we go about our lives, we gather more and more clothes to place in our emotional suitcase. Many times, the emotions we pack away are not happy ones: hurt, disappointment, sadness, pain. Then, instead of being something that helps us get from point A to point B, the suitcase becomes baggage. It weighs us down and hinders our travels, coloring our worldview and tainting our response to new relationships.

One of the significant vows we make in a marriage is to honor, love, and care for, in sickness and in health, till death do us part. That phrase has an even deeper meaning to me.

I've noticed many people move away after a divorce or breakup, as if new surroundings might lessen the pain of the split. After all, places and things remind us of others. Even a song can take you back to a particular place and time and person. Think of Ingrid Bergman saying "Play it once, Sam" in *Casablanca*, and you'll get my meaning.

People search for new environments so that they will not be reminded of a painfully failed relationship. But sometimes even a change of view cannot lessen the pain. You pick your friends, but not your family. What do you do when your mother or father will not talk to you? What do you do when a loved one acts as if you are already dead? Which is worse, a family member that has died, or one that treats you as if you have?

I am still searching for the answers. However, I do know that death brings a certain relief. While my father was alive, I always hoped we would fix our relationship and resume the closeness we shared for a short while. But his wife, Viola, would never allow that to happen. I do not blame her for our problems, only for not allowing us to find a solution. She and I had a stupid tiff during one of their visits about how much time was needed to get to the airport before a flight. I assured her I would get them to the airport in plenty of time. After that she refused to have anything to do with me or my wife, Rosann. To this day I believe it was an excuse to prevent me, a Johnny-come-lately, from supplanting her two children, who were fourteen and sixteen years my junior.

While John lived, there was always hope. Hope springs eternal. But once he died, my hope died with him.

I am as flawed as any other human being, full of weaknesses and shortcomings. But I also have my strengths: intelligence, strong work ethic, resourcefulness, loyalty, and deep caring. However, none of these things matter in a relationship when your efforts are not reciprocated. You cannot change others. You can only change yourself. It does not matter how sincere or well-meaning you are.

It took me a very long time to figure that out. I guess I am still naive when it comes to people. But it's not as if I have led an isolated life. On the contrary, in my forty-eight years with the military and airlines, I have traveled to every continent on the globe, served in war zones, and seen firsthand the best and worst of mankind. Yet I never lost faith in my own ability to affect the outcome of a personal issue. How wrong I was. So how did things get so bad? How did things go so wrong with my family? For those answers I need to go back to the beginning, for this really is the story of my life.

CHAPTER 2

"Butch"

I was born John Patrick Aliano on November 10, 1953. Several significant events occurred that year: The Korean War ended; Sir Edmund Hillary climbed Mount Everest; Chevrolet introduced the Corvette to the American public. Even the day, November 10, is historically important as the US Marine Corps's birthday. But I would not learn this fact until forty years later after serving in the US Air Force.

Of lesser significance, and with little fanfare, I entered the world as the first and only product of John Aliano and Lillian Michaud's union. John was a twenty-year-old machinist of Italian and Irish descent. Lillian was nineteen, of French-Canadian stock, and could trace her family genealogy back to Aroostook County, Maine, and beyond to France itself.

My parents met in central Connecticut while Lillian was visiting one of her cousins who happened to live in my father's hometown of Bristol. My mother was very pretty and very spirited. In later years, she always reminded me of Lucille Ball.

My father was the third son and the last of four children. As the baby of the family, I am sure his brothers and sister thought he was treated like a favorite and, therefore, got away with more than *they* ever could.

And, heightening these feelings of favoritism even more, John suffered severely from polio at a young age. He spent over a year recovering in a hospital bed. The physical therapy sessions were extremely painful, and it wasn't certain whether John would ever walk again, let alone live a full and normal life. John eventually recovered, but the polio left him with a severely curved spine shaped much like a humpback.

While my father may have received special attention from his parents due to his debilitating disease, instead of becoming spoiled and lazy, he hardened into a driven young man. Anxious to prove to anyone and everyone that he was as good as any other boy, my father played sports, enjoyed the great outdoors, and, as a teenager, wooed my mother until she married him.

Unfortunately, their marriage was not to last. My parents initially lived with John's parents, and in later talks with my mother, she seemed to feel that my father's parents did not approve of her.

My parents suffered stresses and strains, as there are in any marriage, which led to fierce arguments. Their strong personalities did not help matters. They were headstrong and had quick tempers. As I found out many years later, Lillian expected absolute loyalty and was slow to forgive.

My father, having been hardened by his childhood disease, was rarely inclined to back down. It may be unkind to say he had a chip on his shoulder, but who would react differently to having their health stolen at such a tender age? John always felt, whether he realized it or not, that he had something to prove. This made him a difficult person to endure the next forty years, until he finally started to relax in retirement.

Regardless, there was a natural fire in both of my parents that made their relationship difficult at best. I was born about two years after they married, and when I was about a year old, my folks had a particularly fierce argument. Years later I learned some of the details. Suffice it to say, my father questioned whether my mother was committed to him and the marriage.

To his credit, rather than stay in a deteriorating situation, my father decided to leave for a while. He moved from Connecticut to

California to work as a machinist in the aviation industry. His self-imposed exile only lasted six months. When he returned, he learned my mother had moved with me to her parents' house in Lindenhurst, New York, on Long Island.

My father contacted my mother and tried to reestablish their relationship, but I was told she spurned all his advances. My maternal grandfather, Edmund, my "Papé," tried his best to facilitate the reconciliation, but it was not to be. They divorced shortly thereafter, and John settled back where he had been born and raised in Bristol, and my mother started a new life on Long Island.

CHAPTER 3

Nana and Papé

My earliest memories are of the two years I spent living in my grandparents' house on Long Island. It is fascinating now to look back at myself at that very young age. My recollections are almost dreamlike, distorted in the smoky mist of nearly seventy years gone by.

I love old movies from the thirties and forties. Like them, the memories of my earliest years are in black and white. However, unlike any movie I know of, my memories come in snippets, as though looking at individual scenes from various films, a montage. I call it the slideshow of my youth.

My very first recollection is of a Saturday morning when I was two or three years old, and it is a powerful reminder of the stubborn blood running through my veins. My mother liked to sleep in on the weekends, and I have always been an early riser, even as a kid. A tough situation since we were sharing a room in my grandparents' house.

I remember her waking up to have a cigarette. I wanted to light the match, but she wouldn't allow me. So, after she had gone back to sleep, I grabbed the matchbook, struck a match, and proceeded to set the entire book aflame, which I was conveniently holding in my left hand.

After all the screaming and tears, my grandmother, Delina, my "Nana," poured a bowlful of milk and had me soak my injured fingers in it all morning. I was a stubborn and willful child, but I always found peace and acceptance in my grandparents' presence.

I remember my aunts and uncles, Deanne, Barbara, and Duane,

being children and teenagers. My aunt Barbara was less than five years older than me, so we sort of grew up together. I would beat up her girlfriends who came to the house. She would think of trouble to get into, drag me along as an unwitting accomplice, and then swear me to secrecy. Of course, I would tell my nana everything as soon as we got home. Ours was a typical and stormy relationship, usual for young siblings, except she was my aunt.

I remember other cousins coming from out of town to visit on holidays and vacations. We always had a houseful, and everyone always called me "Butch." I was too young to remember otherwise, so I never questioned my name. Later in life, I was told my family did not want to be reminded of my father, so they decided to call me by my nickname. If my mother thought a different name would take away the reminders of John, she was sorely mistaken. I believe I reminded her of him every day of my life; I had so much of his personality in me.

As the years progressed, my grandparents became more like parents than grandparents. My grandfather was a machinist like my father, youthful looking, and about the nicest man I had ever known. He was probably too nice for his own good as people often took advantage of his kind nature. He was a self-taught musician who played the piano, guitar, and ukulele.

As we all are, he was a little vain. He would take me with him as he visited different businesses and would pass me off as his son. I have also inherited much of his personality. I am probably too nice for my own good, and I love to receive compliments for either a job well done or for looking youthful in my later years. The strangest thing is that I inherited his roof-shaking sneeze!

Part of my grandmother is inside me as well. She always made everyone who entered her house feel welcome, as if it were their own home. My children always felt comfortable bringing their friends to our house, so I'd like to think my wife and I learned something from Delina.

My grandmother was incredibly honest. She would not hesitate to tell you what she was thinking, even if it was something you did not want to hear. I have always been the same way, struggling all my life with balancing the right formula of forthrightness, to varied success.

In addition, my grandmother was a wonderful cook, the best I have ever known. She and my grandfather both grew up in rural Aroostook County, Maine, one of thirteen children each. There was rarely enough money for store-bought food, so most everything was caught, raised, or grown on the farm.

Sunday dinner at Nana and Papé's house was a major event. Everything was homemade. Nana would bring out plate after plate of the most delicious food. Even if it was something you normally did not like, you would ask for seconds at my grandmother's table.

After the main meal was finished and everyone's bellies were full to bursting, we would find a couch or chair to take a nap on as our stomachs rested. Then, in an hour or so, Nana would bring out the desserts: pies, cakes, cookies, pudding, all homemade along with coffee, tea, and even Postum, a noncaffeinated hot drink so we kids could be like the grown-ups.

When you sat down to dinner at Nana's, you did not expect to get up for at least a couple of hours. Nana taught us that the best part of the bread is the crust, meat bones are meant to be gnawed, and food always tastes better if it comes off someone else's plate!

Dear Nana, like my mother, was also a lifelong smoker and died of cancer while I was in air force pilot training. She was the family matriarch, the glue that held it all together. The family splintered badly after she died, attacking each other at will and vying for what little was left to my grandfather.

Edmund soldiered on for another five or six years, but I don't think his heart was in it. Much of the life went out of him when Delina died. Those closest to him said he died of a broken heart while watching his family become selfish and spiteful after his wife's passing. I loved my grandparents dearly and earnestly miss the warm cocoon of their affection. In this very chaotic world, Nana and Papé were my harbor and, for a time, sheltered me from the tribulations to come.

CHAPTER 4

Richard Hess Jr.

When my mother moved us into my grandparents' house, the first thing my grandfather did was drop her off at a business center, telling her not to come home until she found a job.

She quickly landed a secretarial position in a lawyer's office, which was rather important to our future as she met her next husband there. My grandfather-to-be, Richard Hess Sr., owned his own bakery and used the services of my mother's employer. It wasn't long before he introduced his son, Richard Hess Jr., to my mother.

Here was a young lad fresh out of army service as a tank commander. He had the frightening duty of driving his armored unit across "ground zero" after an above-ground nuclear blast in the American Southwest.

After completing his tour of duty, Richard came home to Long Island, where he soon met my mother, a beautiful woman with a young son in need of a father. I don't know if you can call it an arranged marriage in the traditional sense, but from later conversations, I learned that everyone around them thought it was a logical and sensible thing to do. Remember, this was the mid-fifties, where young divorcées with children lived with difficult social stigmas.

When I was four, my mother married for the second time. I remember the reception, but when I asked about it later in life, I was told it was my aunt's wedding. Richard and Lillian went on a honeymoon with little Butch in tow. We went to Niagara Falls and the Howe Caverns in upstate New York.

I remember the falls being so awesome in their terrible power. We donned rain gear and took a boat ride to the base of the falls just as in the 1953 movie *Niagara* starring Marilyn Monroe.

We went to a small bridge that jutted out over the river above the falls. My new father thought to pick me up so I could have a better view. I screamed bloody murder. He was far too new in my four-year-old life to have that kind of trust.

My last memory of that trip was the visit to the Howe Caverns. Truly remarkable were the large caverns, with their stalactite and stalagmite formations. Just before we returned to the surface, our guide led us into a small, narrow dead-end cave. Then he turned out the lights. I reached out to grab my mother's skirt, but when the lights came on, I was holding on to a total stranger with my death grip. Ah, the dark, terrorizing fears of a four-year-old.

We moved two or three times the first year before settling down, and we lived next to a junkyard for a very short time. What a great place for a young lad to explore! Thank goodness the proprietor did not have a guard dog. On weekend mornings I would get up early and ask my mother if I could go outside to play. Her legs always hurt her, so she would make me sit on them while she slept before releasing me to my adventures.

I also remember living near a large storm drain with very steep and slick sides. One day there was a big commotion in the house, and we all rushed out to see our family cat down in the drain, struggling to climb the steep sides. She was not successful, and there was nothing any of us could do to save her.

I'll never forget the way she looked: wet, tired, and on the verge of exhaustion. I did not stay until she died, but I understood what had happened. Even at a very young age, life was beginning to show me some of her cruel lessons—nothing lasts forever, things are not always fair, and sometimes the ones you love leave. It was only the beginning of a lifetime of these lessons. Thankfully, not all of them were cruel.

All in all, I never thought my earliest years were so different from other kids. I did find that I spent a lot of time alone due to certain circumstances, namely where I lived and Richard Hess's bakery business. Like any kid, I wanted the love and attention of those around me, but I was never at a loss to entertain myself. This discipline would serve me very well in later years as an air force pilot.

CHAPTER 5

West Islip

We settled into a nice Cape Cod house on McElroy Street in 1958 and went about the business of making it a home. For a little boy, I thought the house was huge. I had my own large bedroom, there was a full basement to play in, and the yard was spacious enough to throw a football. The surrounding area was quite rural with lots of woods to explore and plenty of ponds and lakes to go fishing. This was going to be a great place to live.

I started kindergarten that fall and immediately discovered the expectation for neighborhood new kids—I would need to find my place in the pecking order by fighting most of the other boys. Maybe this was not going to be so great after all.

I remember one boy, Steven, who lived just a couple of houses down from ours. I got off the school bus one afternoon and immediately Steven wanted to fight me. I would not turn five until November of that year. Amazing how I went from being a three-year-old terror to a four-year-old coward. I just did not want to fight this stranger, with whom I had no issue at all.

Steven advanced on me, swinging away with all he had. I continued backing up and protecting my face with my forearms. Surprisingly, Steven kept making faces as if striking my arms was hurting his hands. I was scuttling backward, trying to ward off his blows, crying my little eyes out at the horror of my predicament while all the other neighborhood boys surrounded us like buzzards around a dying animal.

Finally, unable to take it anymore, flush with adrenaline, and desperate to end this torture, I wrapped my arms around Steven's neck and squeezed for all I was worth. Crying uncontrollably, I would have ripped his head from his torso if I'd had the strength. Looking back, the situation reminds me of Ralph in *A Christmas Story*, when he finally stands up to the neighborhood bully.

In my case, no parent came to my rescue. Steven croaked uncle and most of the kids left me alone for a long while after that. I think they thought I was a little crazy. Perhaps I was, but I had also learned a valuable lesson: A great defense is to go on the offense, to attack the attacker. In many situations I would face in later life, both physical and emotional, I learned that one could turn a situation to one's advantage simply by refusing to act defensively, forcing one's opponent to defend himself instead.

I was learning the realities of New York streets even there in the quiet suburbs. Just walking one street over placed you at the mercy of an entirely different gang of boys. Some were nicer than others, but I guess they were all concerned with protecting their turf, that little piece of real estate they called their own. Don't we all do that in life, covet what we see and try to guard it against being taken from us?

Eventually I started making friends. Tommy Bentley and his brother Jeff lived across the street, and we had many years of fun and adventure together. In fact, Tommy and I stay in touch to this day. He was quite a weight lifter in his teens and eventually became a lineman for LILCO, the local electric power company.

Jeff was always mechanically inclined. His favorite objects of attention were Volkswagen Beetles. He ran his own automotive repair shop until his recent retirement. Jeff and I hung around together, playing sports (handball was our favorite), camping out, and eventually chasing girls.

Mrs. Bentley was an amusing and memorable woman. She would

bustle about the house, telling us kids what to do. As soon as I entered, she would ask a dozen questions about my family, thereby draining me of all useful information. She was a very good cook, and in the summer, she brewed the most outstanding iced tea with mint leaves grown in her own garden. Since no one could afford air-conditioning, you counted yourself truly blessed to be invited to partake of Mrs. Bentley's refreshing iced tea during those long hot summer days.

I also became friends with John and Steve Rostrum, who lived one block over from us. My mother became very close friends with their mother, and to this day we call their parents Uncle Jack and Aunt Jan. Eventually they moved to a beautiful little bungalow on the Great South Bay, where I learned to love boating, sailing, fishing, and the beaches of Long Island.

John, Steve, and I had sleepovers, went fishing, and played youth football together for several years. In fact, we were part of the championship team three years in a row. I played right halfback and then quarterback for the Jets, namesake of the New York pro team. One year I scored more touchdowns than any other member of our league.

John became an electrician and is still around, but Steve succumbed to cancer at too young an age. It was another of life's lessons, that the world can be both random and unfair.

I later went on to run junior varsity track. I never really thought of myself as being the strong, athletic type, but sports were an integral part of my life as a kid in New York. It was a safe way to prove yourself to the other boys. Don't get me wrong, the competition was fierce. But I proved to be a swift, wiry, and persistent opponent, qualities that would serve me well later in life.

Along with my sports successes—which developed my habit for fitness, one which proved crucial to working off stress and managing the rigors of military flying—came a slowly developing confidence. As an air force pilot, that self-confidence was often the difference between success and failure, or worse.

CHAPTER 6

Growing Up in New York

Shortly after we moved to West Islip my mother became pregnant. She gave birth to Timothy, and five years after that, Raymond. As the oldest, I got to keep my own room. Such was the hierarchy in the Hess house. Thank goodness for being the oldest.

I always loved having my brothers. We are all five years apart, so growing up together really wasn't much competition. We moved in different circles, saw each other at home, and sometimes played games or sports together in the neighborhood. Tim and Ray were good brothers. They let me be the traditional older brother, and we covered for each other as best we could.

I remember powerful snowstorms that paralyzed the adult world for days but gave us kids a never-ending wonderland in which to play. We constructed snow forts and had endless snowball fights, built huge snowmen, and spent countless hours sledding down a nearby hill. Long Island was proving to be a fun place to live year-round.

We traveled a lot on weekends to visit relatives. Sunday family dinners, whether at our house or someone else's, were usually fun and interesting. Nana and Papé would come over and our grandfather would teach us boys how to play chess and many card games. Edmund was a cigar and pipe smoker, and to this day the right kind of tobacco smell instantly transports me back to those Sunday afternoons in my mother's living room with my Papé.

I was also getting to know the extended Hess family. They were nice enough, just different from my mother's family. My grandfather was a severe man, the kind you were careful to show respect to. They lived in an old house behind a big hospital in Rockville Centre with a huge yard to play in and a quaint general store across the street.

My father had a brother, Uncle Buddy, who was mentally handicapped. They told me he had a difficult birth and that the doctor had to use implements to bring him into this world. I learned much about the basic goodness of the human spirit by observing my uncle.

Uncle Buddy spent his adult life in and out of mental institutions on Long Island, to include the infamous Pilgrim State Hospital. He was slow-witted and would often latch on to an idea then repeat some statement over and over in stubborn single-mindedness. But he was also the gentlest soul I have ever known. There wasn't a mean bone in his body. In fact, my uncle often showed me the bruises he received at the hands of the other detainees. Yet he would never strike back, not even to defend himself.

Uncle Buddy must have found this world a remarkably cruel and confusing place. Not having the capacity to understand or adapt, he was trapped in his damaged mind until a natural or unnatural act sent him on to the next life. Richard and Lillian separated after less than ten years, and I am sorry to say I never knew what became of my uncle, but I think of him now and again.

I have since met many people like Uncle Buddy and truly believe the Lord has selected them for a higher purpose. More often than not, they are the gentlest of souls, trusting simply and completely. In my later life as an airline pilot, those with Down syndrome have come up to me while deplaning and given me the most wonderful hugs before exiting the aircraft. Perhaps their often-childlike nature helps remind us of how He really wants us to be.

While we lived with Richard Hess, he had us attend church and Sunday school at a local Presbyterian parish. I enjoyed the Sunday school classes and made many good friends. I remember one girl, Alice, who had an above-ground swimming pool in her backyard. We had many fun pool parties in the summer, and I even remember kissing her at the end of one of them. My first kiss. We were only fourteen years old.

My Nana and Papé were lifelong Catholics, and we would often attend services with them. It was both fascinating and disorientating because the Mass was still conducted in Latin at that time. So many intricate procedures: stand up, sit down, cross yourself, kneel, recite the liturgy, etc. It was very different from the Protestant service.

An interesting note—since my mother's parents were Catholic and my mother was raised as such, my nana asked my mother to have us converted once she divorced Richard Hess. So, at the age of fifteen, I was schooled and then converted into the Catholic Church. I like the feeling of continuity the Church gives me, but honestly, I haven't forgotten my Presbyterian upbringing. I still talk to God, one-on-one, every day.

I don't think I am unique having experienced both services, but I must admit I like one particular thing above all else from my Presbyterian childhood. I sincerely like the concept of a personal, one-on-one relationship with God. As I have grown older, I find myself talking to God multiple times each day. I give thanks before each meal. I often ask Him to keep me safe and to protect my loved ones. I also ask for His intervention in all the crazy things I see happening in the world today, whether it be the tribulations of partisan politics or worldwide terrorism. There is so much to pray for.

Looking back, Richard Hess was an interesting character to live with. The very first memory I have of the house in West Islip was playing in the big yard, which was surrounded by a border of young hedges.

One day I tried to leap over a section, overestimating how high or far my legs would carry me, and proceeded to fall into the bush, breaking off a branch.

My stepfather stormed out the back door, dragged me into the kitchen, placed me over his knee, and spanked me until I peed my pants . . . again. I was then sent to my room without supper so I could reflect on my transgression. This was the beginning of corporal punishment on a regular basis. No infraction was too small. I remember one incident that has left me shaking my head to this day.

Richard was a baker like his father before him. Typical of the trade, he would rise long before the sun and come home shortly after lunch. While in kindergarten, I stayed home sick one day. My stepfather came home, marched into my bedroom, took off his belt, and proceeded to whip me.

I will never forget his words: "That's just in case you're faking it." I was not even five years old yet. I learned quickly not to antagonize my new father.

During this time, my parents contacted my biological father, John, in Connecticut, asking him if he would consider giving me up for adoption. John consulted his father but was left to make his own decision. And so he agreed, and I took Richard's name. John told me later he thought it would be in my best interest. Living in another state, there was no way he could have known otherwise.

My mother and Richard fought constantly at night. They were vicious, loud arguments I listened to while hiding in the dark sanctuary of my upstairs bedroom. My mother usually ended the argument by storming out of the house and driving around until she cooled off. She would continue this habit for the rest of her life.

I had forgotten that I even had another father besides Richard. When I was fourteen, my mother explained that John was my real father and that she was planning on leaving Richard. For a while, I did not want to be with Richard even though my brothers always did. The new knowledge left me confused and even more afraid of him.

When my mother kicked Richard out of the house, he responded by cutting off all financial support. In very short order, she finished high school with a GED, completed a business degree, and went to work. My mother was too proud to accept welfare, so we all pitched in and did what we could. Some weeks we ate better than others, but we always managed to get by.

At the age of fourteen I bought her a car with money I had saved from a paper route. In fact, I have been continuously employed in one form or another since I was twelve years old. As the old saying goes, "Necessity is the mother of invention." I understand and appreciate the drive that comes when you have no other choice. Later in life, I always pondered how to teach my children this discipline without making them suffer the hardships.

After my mother's second divorce and while she worked, Richard would often come to the house and visit us children since his work schedule allowed him afternoons off. He always owned his own bakery, first in East Islip and then in Brightwaters and Brentwood, not too far away. He would take a nap, make dinner, and then leave when my mother came home from work.

One day when I was fifteen, he was at the house with us three boys. My mother had a miniature dog of a breed I have since forgotten. My brother Raymond, just five years old, was teasing the dog. It had a bed that looked more like a wicker igloo, with a small opening at its front. Every time my brother reached his hand toward the opening, the dog would try to nip him.

I told Raymond, "Leave the dog alone."

Of course he ignored me, and after a couple of times I tapped him lightly on the butt with my foot to get him to quit. My father was just a few feet away making a sandwich. He immediately dropped everything, stepped up to me, and punched me hard in the shoulder. After ten years of his abuse, I had had enough.

I grabbed both his wrists. Richard struggled mightily to free himself, but he couldn't budge. I thought he might knee me in the groin, so I shifted one leg to protect the jewels. I pulled him in close until our noses nearly touched and said, "If you ever touch me again, I'll freaking kill you."

That was the last time Richard Hess ever touched me. Now that I look back, I don't remember him being the same way with my two brothers, which makes me wonder why he wanted to adopt me in the first place. He gave me his name, forever losing the opportunity to give it to one of his own. Go figure.

Even my mother had had enough of his shenanigans. One afternoon we were all at home, once again in the kitchen preparing a meal. My father and mother were having a conversation, but no one else was listening. Without warning my mother started screaming at Richard. She beat him backward toward the back door, and I immediately took position behind her, backing her up. Richard took one look into my eyes and simply put his hands up to protect his face, not daring to strike back.

Tommy Bentley was waiting for me on the back porch. The expression on his face, as he saw my mother literally beating my father out of the house, with me standing behind her, was precious indeed. The funny thing is that none of my friends knew my parents were getting divorced until two years after he left.

I have always found it so hard to talk to people about certain things. There are just some things you can't share with anyone except the closest of friends. I remember my mother telling me, "You can count on one hand the number of true friends you have."

She was so right. It's difficult to expose your deepest fears or concerns to anyone you worry might betray you. I've always said it's easy to be a friend when times are good, but oh so hard when times are bad. That's when a friend's true colors show, when the chips are down. A joke I once heard is that a good friend will bail you out of jail. A great friend will sit beside you in the cell saying, "Damn, that was fun!"

We are all shaped by our environment. My childhood had plenty of ups and downs and helped mold me into who I am today. Because of my own experiences, I truly believe I understand the value of friendship and loyalty. Once, when we were having an argument, I told my mother I was a good friend to have in a storm. I hope she believed me.

In the meantime, I tried to be a good son to both my parents, but it was very difficult. For a time, I worked at the bakery. In fact, several of my friends met future wives through a friendship I developed with Terri, the girl who worked at the cash register.

But my father was determined to use his children as weapons to hurt my mother. The last straw came when my father accused us boys of stealing money from his store. We suffered the embarrassment of going to the local police station for a lie-detector test to prove our innocence. It was more than even I could stand. My naivete was long gone, and I made the painful decision to have nothing further to do with Richard Hess. I was seventeen and no longer had a father.

CHAPTER 7

Friends

One of the lessons I learned fast was how important your friends can be in your life. In many ways, your friends become your family. We all want certain things. The basics are food and shelter, physical security, and a sense of belonging. In fact, these are the lower tiers of Maslow's hierarchy of needs. Usually, it is your home and family that provide these needs when you are young. However, as you approach your teen years, especially near a big city like New York, your friends truly take on a greater importance. Mine were no different.

We called ourselves "Richie and the Poor Boys." We had our own special greeting and handshake and protected each other through the high school years. The group was named after Richie Speena. The "Poor Boys" were me, Mike Tornabene, Joe Tornabene, Mitch Kofski, George and Greg Vallone, Steve Timpone, and a few others.

I suppose you could call us a gang, but we were more like a social club, only wanting to support each other. Two of us had cars. We would work, pool our money, and then spend it communally to pay for gas and get us into dance parties, which were common every weekend during the summer months. We really did a good job covering for each other, because New York can be a frightening and dangerous place if no one is watching your back.

We all tried our best to find desirable girls to date, but dating in New York was like navigating a minefield. If you said the wrong thing to a girl, her boyfriend might track you down and get in your face. If a girl was available, her ex-boyfriend would do everything, including the threat of physical violence, in his power to keep prospective suitors away. I suppose the logic was "If I can't have her, no one can" or "If I can't have her, I'll keep everyone else away, so she'll have no choice but to come back to me."

I probably owe George Vallone my life. I had dated a girl named Helen for a short time, but she broke up with me and moved on to the kid brother of one of our gym teachers. He and a jock friend caught up to George and me one afternoon as we were walking home. The jock got out of the car and started talking trash. George, who was a big solid football player himself, immediately started giving it back.

"Excuse me. Are you talking to me? Are you talking to me? You got something to say, say it to me." Robert De Niro had nothing on George. That jock backpedaled into the car, and we never heard a peep from them again.

Thank you, George, for guarding my back.

Another time we had managed to get some beer and were comfortably buzzed on a late Saturday night. I was in a local hangout, a pizza joint, with my arm around a well-endowed young lady when her ex-boyfriend walked in. He was from the next town over and had a nasty reputation. I was about to be in trouble.

Another friend was with me, Tommy Keiffer. Tommy lived around the corner from me, and he and I had an on-again, off-again friendship for twenty years. Thank God we were on-again that night. All I remember seeing through hazy eyes was Tommy putting his arm around the guy's shoulder and talking quietly while he walked him out the door. A few minutes later, Tommy walked back in alone as if nothing had happened. I never asked, and Tommy never told me, what he said or did to make the guy go away.

Thank you, Tommy, for guarding my back.

Another good friend from my youth was Pat Walsh. I met Pat when I was just four years old. He lived across the street from my

Nana and Papé, and he was a great guy: outgoing and smart but also always a schemer. From one day to the next you never knew what trouble he would drag you into. We stayed in touch until he retired and moved to upstate New York to live on a remote property in the mountains. But before he left, Pat dated my wife's sister Marie long enough for me to meet and start dating Rosann. It is because of Pat that I found the love of my life.

Thank you, Patrick Thomas Walsh.

Tommy Keiffer died of skin cancer in his late thirties. Joe Tornabene died in his sleep at a young age of unknown causes. A couple of others ended up in institutions for various reasons. I stay in touch with Mike Tornabene and Mitch Kofski on a regular basis to this day. The relationships from my youth hold a special meaning as they are a thread that goes back to the beginning. And for a very important time, these friends gave me the safety and sense of belonging I so sorely needed.

We also shared our faith, which can be absent in teenagers. Before heading out for a weekend of fun, our "gang" would usually go to a nearby Catholic church or hospital for the early Saturday-morning Mass. I look back now and appreciate that constant tie to God that protected us as we gallivanted all over New York City and Long Island.

As high school was ending, it was time to pursue Maslow's higher levels of needs: esteem and self-actualization. I graduated in the top 5 percent of my class, qualified for a Regents Scholarship, and was accepted to several colleges. My interests were marine biology and oceanography, so I decided to attend the Merchant Marine Academy at Fort Schuyler in New York City. It would not be far from home, but it was time to leave the nest.

CHAPTER 8

Spreading My Wings

That summer following high school graduation was quite an eye-opener. I had a short break to enjoy the weather, the beaches, and my friends before it was time to leave all that was familiar for the pre-academic summer camp for plebes (first-year students) entering the academy.

The first rule in the military is: Shit rolls downhill, and plebes are at the bottom of the pile. We were up with the sun and dead to the world by the time it set. There was plenty of good old-fashioned PT (physical training): running, calisthenics, swimming, and rowing. And, though nothing like getting in physical shape, there was much more. I was only seventeen and about to get a graduate-level introduction to hazing and abuse.

The upperclassmen ran the summer program and were expected to maintain discipline and decorum throughout the school year. This was 1971. The Vietnam War was winding down and US servicemen had received brutal treatment at the hands of their captors. It was important that we quickly develop thick skin, strong bodies, and even tougher minds for the realities of military service to come. Besides, lowerclassmen had suffered pain and abuse at the hands of their upperclassmen since the time of the first military academies. It was a rite of passage, something everyone went through before being accepted, much the same as pledging for a fraternity.

Of course, we had to run everywhere and stand at attention whenever addressed. But the real fun began at night while the rest of the world slept. Somewhere around midnight the hallway lights would suddenly turn on and upperclassmen would throw our dorm room doors open, screaming for us to get dressed in our dress whites and "fall out." Then we were marched into the common-area latrines, where all the hot-water faucets in the sinks and showers were turned on full bore until the room was so thick with steam you could not see the other end of the room.

A favorite torture position was the "brace," where you stand at attention with every muscle in your body rigidly tightened. Imagine it is summertime, the middle of the night, and you are roused from a deep sleep, clothed in a full-dress uniform, crowded into a 120-degree steam bath, forced to stand in a brace with every muscle quivering while your tormentors scream continuous venom at you. Worst of all, you are told you had better not let the guy next to you hit the floor if he fainted. So here you are, trying to stay alive, alert, and not faint yourself, but more worried that your neighbor might hit the tiles before you could reach out and grab him!

Those summer weeks passed quickly enough, and soon we were engrossed in our studies. Most of the first-year courses were no different from those required at any university. I took some oceanography courses and worked part-time in the science labs. I went home most weekends to my family and friends. Life was pretty good.

My roommate was Black, from New York City, and an engineering major. I was intrigued with him for several reasons. He would describe spending hours tracing systems in the four-hundred-foot-long training ship the school had tied up at our dock and which sailed to Europe in the summers. We all had to do campus security details, which included patrols on the ship. It was a fascinating yet darkly foreboding place on the night watch.

My roommate also taught me a bit about human nature. I grew up in a mostly White town. Out of 640 high school graduates, only a handful were Black or Hispanic. This was my chance to satisfy a strong curiosity. What were others like, those who looked different than me? I found out, of course, that they were no different. They had idiosyncrasies, hopes, fears, likes, dislikes. They possessed all the things that make us wonderful and terrible. I was glad for the chance to confirm what I already knew in my heart.

The first school year passed quickly. Honestly, I was a bit bored with school and unhappy with being away from home, and I don't think I was ready for the rigid military system. I decided to transfer to Stony Brook, a large university on the North Shore of Long Island. I would move back home and commute to school daily.

If Fort Schuyler underwhelmed me then Stony Brook had the opposite effect. This was a big school with thousands of students. Many of my classes were in huge lecture halls with hundreds of students per class, and I had the feeling that I was just a nameless face among thousands of other nameless faces. I didn't know anyone, and I drove home after my last class each day, denying myself a chance to get to know my peers. I also took some difficult classes. After receiving a D in a chemistry class, I decided it wasn't for me. I don't think I even finished the semester. I was learning that I didn't like failure, but I was also having a hard time finding what motivated me. If my heart wasn't in it, I just didn't give it my best effort. I was still searching for what made me tick.

I got a job that winter working for GEICO. They had just built a large regional office and there was plenty of work to do. I figured I would work for six months and then go back to school. I ended up in the computer department and liked it enough to change my major when I transferred to the local community college. I liked the subjects; they held my interest, and I was finally applying myself totally with excellent results. My grades were nearly straight As, and the school year flew by.

More important than the work at GEICO, or even the renewed motivation I found, were the people I met during that time. In the first week I met David Brenner, an offset printer. David was a wiry, sometimes loud, but always full-of-energy workmate. After a playful boxing match that ended with David in a garbage bin, we quickly became best friends. He was an avid athlete who rekindled my love for baseball, handball, racquetball, and bowling, and he came from a well-to-do Jewish family. Yet David stubbornly felt compelled to seek his own path. We are as close as brothers to this day, and I believe this shared independent spirit is the reason.

During that year I also met my future wife, who is three years younger. Her older sister, Marie, who was just a year younger than me, was going with her friends to a popular nightspot for her birthday, as we could drink in New York at eighteen. I happened to be there that Saturday night with Pat Walsh, the big Irish kid who grew up across the street from my grandparents in Lindenhurst. He has always been a hoot to be around: loud, obnoxious, full of inappropriate jokes. He's an avid hunter and the best shot, bar none, of anyone I've ever met. Pat taught me it's okay to laugh, even at yourself, and to never take things too seriously.

That night at the club, Marie found Pat sitting on the edge of the bandstand during a break in the music. Thinking he was part of the band, she struck up a conversation that eventually led to them dating. I liked to tease Marie on her birthday every year that it was the anniversary of her getting drunk and picking up one of my friends. Pat and I were both nineteen, but for some silly reason we told Marie we were twenty-one.

Anyway, I got set up with a couple of her girlfriends because I had a car and Pat did not, but it never lasted more than a few dates. Then one day Pat and I went to Marie's house and met her family. When I walked in, Rosann was in the kitchen with one of her girlfriends studying a nursing textbook. I walked in and started talking to them about their schoolwork. I learned Rosann's first impression of me later.

She told her girlfriend, "You know, I'd never go out with a guy like that. He's too much of a flirt!"

Well, a couple of weeks later, she changed her tune. Marie and Pat were not getting along very well. Their mom, Josephine, asked Marie, "Why don't you go out with Richie? He seems like a nice boy."

"I can't do that," Marie responded. "He's Pat's best friend."

Rosann piped up, "Well, set him up with me."

"You can't go out with him either. He's twenty-one and you're only sixteen. Besides, you're already going out with Bobby."

Not to be deterred, Rosann picked up the phone and broke up with Bobby that very day. The next night was our first date. So where did I take her? To an ex-girlfriend's house, because I was friends with her brother! I remember our first kiss good night. For the first time in my life, someone seemed to fit exactly right. More importantly, I seemed to fit. Rosann's family was typically Italian: passionate, close, supportive, with a large extended family. Her father was a retired navy corpsman who stitched young warriors back together after they had been torn asunder on the beaches of Guadalcanal and Iwo Jima. I learned a lot from Prosper Ambrico, and for a long time, he was more like a father to me than anyone else.

It wasn't that there was no man at home. In fact, my mother met husband number three, Frank Loy, where she worked. They were both divorced, he once and she twice. They married just as I finished my first year of college. He was very good for my mother and my kid brothers, but he seemed at a loss on how to deal with me, since I was quite a bit older than his own son and daughter. Ours was a stormy relationship. Frank always took my mother's side in any argument, never staying neutral, and I had not yet learned that sometimes less is more. We both found that we could keep the peace if we just avoided each other. It was not the best situation, but it was livable.

Frank was a quiet man, did not say much and mostly stayed in the background. He suffered severely from diabetes. The doctors were never able to stabilize his medication. Frank loved to fish but we always worried about him being on the water alone, so one of us kids usually went with him. It wasn't unusual for him to go into diabetic shock, requiring us to load the boat and drive home. My brother Tim drove Frank home safely more than once even though he was only fourteen or fifteen years old.

When I turned twenty, I started feeling restless. I am sure there were many reasons: I was still living at home where the relationships were strained; I had met my wife-to-be and knew that I loved her; I felt the need to strike out on my own. Many of my friends still lived at home but I was ready to leave. I remember being frustrated with how I felt. I used to say that for every two steps forward I felt like I was taking one step back. That's a line from a Paula Abdul song, isn't it? She must have heard me say it years ago.

I had an acquaintance that had enlisted in the air force and was waiting for her boot camp date. I went down to the local recruiting office with her one day. I remember sitting in a chair, talking with the recruiter, and, the next thing I knew, I had a pen in my hand and an enlistment contract in front of me. I signed it, barely understanding what I was doing, then felt sick to my stomach. What had I done? There was no turning back now.

I should not have worried. The Lord was watching over me and pointing me in the right direction. I had scored in the top 1 percent of the aptitude test and Uncle Sam wanted me! I was offered a four-year scholarship to attend the Air Force Academy in Colorado Springs. However, I had already completed two years of college and knew I wanted to get married soon, so I thought another four years spent getting an undergraduate degree would be wasteful. But not everyone who knew me thought I was acting sane.

Howard Roseman, my mother's lawyer, had two daughters but no son. He and I would go to dinner then attend some sports event like father and son. He was good to me during those teenage years, and I appreciate his generosity more than I can ever express. My mother called Howard, and he invited me to come to his office to talk. I told him about my plans to enter the air force. He was horrified when I told him I had signed a general enlistment with no job guarantee. Why, they could make me a cook or a janitor!

Howard didn't hesitate. He asked me, "Where do you want to go to school? You choose. If you want to go to law school, I will get you into my alma mater. If you want to go to medical school, I know the director of the State University of New York system. Just finish your degrees and we will worry about paying me back after you graduate."

What an offer! Who could say no to that?

I could. I told him, "Howard, that's an incredible offer. Thank you so very much. But I want to strike out on my own, so I'm going into the military to make my own way."

Howard owed me nothing, but he offered me everything. I went on to achieve so much in the military, including advanced degrees. Later, when I would go home and visit him, Howard would tell friends I was a good example of him being wrong.

Thank you, Howard, for just being there in my cheering section.

June 1974 was soon upon me. I went to Fort Hamilton in Brooklyn for my entry physical. I along with a hundred other guys lined up like an assembly line in front of an old guy in a lab coat who looked like he should be retired, soaking up rays on a Florida beach rather than poking and probing our bodies in the most cursory way.

"Feet spread apart. Turn your head to the side. Cough. Move on. Next!" How do you fail this thing?

I had entered and left a military academy. I was part of the lottery system when I was nineteen, received a high number, and therefore bypassed the draft. Now I was voluntarily enlisting. What was I thinking? The best part of this process was being given an airline ticket to San Antonio, Texas. This was to be my first flight, and as the saying goes, "the start of a beautiful relationship."

CHAPTER 9

Bars and Stripes

Summertime Basic Training in south Texas. Can you say hot? We were rounded up from the terminal at San Antonio by stern-faced men in crisp uniforms. When we got to Lackland Air Force Base (AFB) we were lined up in military formation. We went *everywhere* in formation. But oh, to see us, all dressed up in every shade and style of civilian dress! We looked like a rainbow. In fact, that is exactly what they called us that first week. I still remember the first cadence we heard from other formations as they passed us by.

"Rainbow, rainbow, don't be blue. My recruiter screwed me too."

Those first weeks were the toughest, trying to do everything the TI (training instructor) wanted while being hustled everywhere and yelled at nearly continuously. But there was no physical abuse this time, just verbal. If you messed up, extra push-ups were the worst that would happen, or perhaps you would be hauled in front of the entire formation for public embarrassment.

The dorms were modern and clean. The PT was reasonable. My fellow "inmates" were a pretty good bunch. The only thing that bothered me was being yelled at all the time—I really did not like that. It stressed me out. I went to sick call, spent two days in the dispensary, and thought seriously about calling it quits. I called Rosann and my mom, but they could not help me on this one. This was one decision I needed to make on my own.

Those two days of peace and quiet did me wonders. I managed to calm down and recommit myself to finish what I had started. I went back to my unit Monday morning and finished the rest of boot camp with no problems. In fact, it turned out to be kind of fun. I enjoyed the PT, even running the track in combat boots! We ran a great obstacle course that I wished we had access to every day, and I shot "expert" with the M16 rifle. I had turned a proverbial corner and was ready for the next challenge.

While in boot camp, I was offered several jobs. Obviously, my high aptitude scores had caught someone's attention. A serious-minded sergeant tried to talk me into accepting an assignment as a combat controller. If I had to do it over again, I'm sure I would jump at such an offer, but I still had selfish motives at that time. I wanted to finish my college education, so I was looking for a job that would support that goal, and either coast was fine by me. They finally offered me a computer operator position at Ent AFB in Colorado Springs, and I said yes. What the heck—Colorado is halfway between the East and West Coast, right?

I reported to Ent AFB and was sent to meet my squadron commander in the Cheyenne Mountain Complex. I was now a part of NORAD (North American Defense Command) and would be working on a new missile-tracking computer. The nuclear blast doors that protected the inner spaces of Cheyenne Mountain were massive, and the buildings inside were mounted on huge springs to absorb shocks. What a place!

But most impressive was my new commander. He was a lieutenant colonel and a very sharp guy. We talked a bit about work, hobbies, and aspirations. One year later, when I went back for a recommendation for a college scholarship, he remembered every detail of our first conversation. I was truly impressed.

I also got a chance to meet another impressive character, General

"Chappy" James. He was the NORAD four-star commander while I was there. A Tuskegee airman, Daniel James flew 101 fighter combat missions in Korea and another 78 in Vietnam. Later, as I came to truly appreciate our pioneering aviators, I was glad for the chance to meet a larger-than-life personality.

Colorado Springs was good duty. The town was still small in 1974, yet there was plenty to do. I only wished it was closer to home and Rosann. We played ice hockey and skied in the winter, then climbed mountains and went spelunking (cave exploring) in the summer. Cripple Creek and Garden of the Gods were regular destinations.

The air force sent me to Gulfport, Mississippi, for computer training. I had a crazy marine for a roommate—thank goodness it was only for a few weeks. We ended up holed up on base as Hurricane Carmen ravaged the Gulf Coast and the New Orleans area. I have never seen the sky so black in the middle of the day. What an awesome yet terrifying sight.

Back in Colorado Springs, it was time to get serious. Rosann and I were to be married in January in New York. I will never forget my nervousness in asking her father for her hand. I had just returned home from Basic Training. I just could not get the words out.

Finally, he nudged me along. "So, you want to marry my daughter?"

"Yes, sir," I answered.

"When do you want to have the ceremony?"

"How about two or three months from now?"

"What's your rush?"

"No rush, Pop. We can put it off a few months if you like." Phew! These Italian fathers were enough to give a young guy a heart attack!

In Colorado, I immersed myself in the job and life in the mountains. One weekend I was exploring the backside of Cave of the Winds, looking for new caves. I was about thirty feet up a sheer rock face when the whole face shifted and gave way. I let go, got my feet underneath me, and fell twenty feet to a shallow rock ledge.

Amazingly, I landed on my feet with no injuries. Then a boulder hit my left leg and snapped the bones six inches above the ankle.

It took the El Paso County Search and Rescue team hours to get me off that mountain. I could feel myself going into shock but willed myself to stay alert. The wail of the ambulance siren brought a flood of tears as the relief of safety washed over me. I ended up in the Air Force Academy hospital for over a month. But it took my bones another six months to knit. It looked like I was going to be married in a cast.

The wedding was a hoot. All my friends and relatives were there, as was Rosann's large extended family, with one exception. My mother was feuding at the time with my godmother, her sister Deanne. She made it clear to me that she would not come to the wedding if I invited my aunt. My nana handed me an envelope from my aunt behind my mother's back that night. When my mother found out, she did not speak to Nana for weeks. I always regretted not having my aunt at my wedding, but I was also starting to see just how hard it was to play the role of a "good son." It would only get worse.

The rest of the short time Rosann and I spent in Colorado Springs was great. It always amazes me to look back at how little we had, and yet how rich we felt. We rented a furnished one-bedroom apartment for $150 a month, utilities included! I took home $250 every two weeks from Uncle Sam, and Rosann was working as a nurse for a salary of $10,000 a year. You could buy a really nice home to raise a family for less than $30,000.

Life was good, but mostly because I had Rosann to come home to every day. We argued some, but mostly we were learning to live as a couple, on our own, away from any family influences.

My scholarship came through about six months after the wedding. We packed our things to visit family in New York before heading to Miami, where I had an ROTC slot awaiting me.

Rosann and I enjoyed our few weeks at home that summer. I spent lots of time with my friends and she was with her mother and sister. The three of them were like the Three Musketeers, going everywhere together. Then in early August we drove to Miami. On the evening we arrived in south Florida, we stopped in Fort Lauderdale to visit one of Rosann's older cousins who had recently moved there from New York.

Rosann's older cousin, Mary, was divorced with two young children. I don't know the whole story. Mary moved to Florida, but soon thereafter decided to move back to New York. We just happened to come along as Mary was packing up and preparing for the move, so we helped her pack their belongings and entertained the kids to ease the stress of multiple moves.

Her daughter was fine. She always seemed to take things in stride. Her son was a bit more upset. He was a special child with some disabilities and always needed a firm hand. I remember taking them to a drive-in zoo in New Jersey one weekend when Rosann and I were dating. It was a blast, including when three rhinos ran directly at our car, splitting left and right at the last minute.

Vito always liked to wrestle. He was incredibly strong for a young boy and sometimes difficult to control. Again, I always used a firm but loving hand with him, and we got along very well.

Anyway, that night in Fort Lauderdale we helped Mary as best we could. She had called another cousin to come down and drive back to New York with her. Mary asked if I would go to the airport and pick him up, and I was happy too.

I had never met Mary's cousin before, but some of Rosann's extended Italian family had a certain reputation for being "connected," if you get my meaning. Who's to say if such a thing is true? But if it *were* true, this guy scared the heck out of me. He was probably less than forty, no more than five foot two or three. He was *very* quiet, the kind of guy that made you nervous because he said nothing and observed everything. We walked into Mary's apartment, where greetings and hugs were exchanged.

The important lesson I was learning from Rosann's family was that when a member was in need, it was our duty to help.

The next day we drove to Miami and started the search for a place to live.

I had never been to Miami before, so I wasn't sure what to expect. It was interesting to say the least. The weather was hot and sticky that August, and the vegetation was lush and tropical compared to Colorado. The University of Miami campus was large but friendly. I was excited to get started.

Little did I know that finding an apartment would be so difficult. We searched the classifieds in the *Miami Herald* and looked at a few apartments, but none seemed to suit our needs. Some were in run-down parts of town; some did not allow pets (we had a dog); one looked more like a retirement home; one had residents that looked like old hippies from the '60s. Finally, we checked out a building just south of the international airport, on a lake, with a pool and a game room. We decided to take it. What a place! Most of the residents were Cuban and spoke Spanish as their first language. The manager had been a sergeant in Batista's army. He was friendly enough, but he carried a machete everywhere around the grounds. I made a vow not to piss him off!

The next order of business was to find Rosann a job. There were plenty of hospitals and clinics but several of them refused to hire anyone who was not bilingual. She finally landed a position at a children's hospital on the west side of Coral Gables, very near the college campus.

The children's hospital was a great job for Rosann, but it also took a lot out of her. As the junior nurse, she was almost always on the midnight shift. So, we did not get to sleep side by side very often. On the nights we did sleep together, I was forever trying to push her out of bed in my sleep, until one night she socked me in the jaw with a left cross that left me sore.

But the hardest part of her job was dealing with sick children who were suffering from cancer or abuse. Rosann always had a caring nature that the parents recognized. Often, when a kid was about to die, they would specifically ask for Rosann to attend to the child. She would come home from those shifts and cry her eyes out. Tough duty for a nurse only nineteen years old.

Now that we were settled, it was time to go to school. I immersed myself in my classes very quickly. I signed up as a computer science major with a minor in mathematics. Again, I was applying myself very well and enjoying the classes. Computer programming and operations seemed archaic then compared to how things are done now. We would write a program in BASIC or Assembly, generate a stack of punch cards for instructions and data, then have an operator run it through the mainframe computer. Everything was cumbersome and time-consuming.

The ROTC attachment I was assigned to turned out to be a dynamic organization. It was run by Colonel Bob Patterson, a Vietnam veteran with quite a story to tell. He flew the RF-101 Voodoo, a reconnaissance version of that venerable "Century Series" fighter. They had the dangerous job of flying over potential targets to gather intelligence that could then be used by fighters and bombers, or they were sent to do damage assessment after an airstrike.

Colonel Patterson was shot down twice, once by a MIG fighter and once by a SAM (surface-to-air missile). On his last shoot down, the rescue helicopter dragged him through the jungle while he held on for dear life at the end of a rescue hoist.

I look back now and see how the good Lord always seemed to put the right person with me just as I needed him. Colonel Patterson was the right person for the job of shaping our mindsets. He was pleasant, approachable, and reasonable, yet he showed us that dangerous duty awaited us. Perhaps most importantly, I sensed from him that you could face these dangers, even suffer greatly because of them, yet survive with your body, mind, and soul intact. I am forever grateful he was there to teach us these important lessons.

College and ROTC kept me busy. Between classes, formations, and sports activities, I had a full schedule. But I also got a chance to get well acquainted with the Miami area. Lord, there was plenty to do. I subscribed to the *Florida Sportsman* and was constantly impressed with how many species there were to hunt and fish. I became a regular on a fishing boat, the *Captain Rudy*, to the point where I was usually mistaken for one of the crew.

Rosann's dad loved to fish. He would find any excuse to get out of New York for a week or two and stay with us. Sometimes I don't know how I got through college for all the time we spent on *Captain Rudy*. But it was nice to have a father figure around to share time with, and we always had a freezer full of fresh fish. I think Prosper Ambrico made up for a lot of what I did without when I was younger.

Thank you, Pop, for giving me your time, and for sharing your passion for the sea.

I was out fishing one weekend afternoon on a local canal when a fellow named Jeff Norman joined me. We introduced ourselves, one thing led to another, and we became good friends. His dad, Lane, was an insurance salesman. He and Jeff lived in a small house nearby. I used to love to go to see Lane while Jeff was at school. We would sit at his dining room table and drink coffee and just talk. I think having grown up without a good father figure made me seek out the time and attention of other older men. It is something I have noticed in myself all my adult life.

Through Jeff I also became friends with "Little Joe" Aspillaga, "Big Nose" Joe (never learned his last name), Little Joe's cousin Phillip, and a fellow named Billy. We would hang out, go fishing and boating, and do all the normal things a group of young men would do.

Little Joe and I are friends to this day, and I visit him whenever I am in south Florida. Joe is from Chile and his ex and current wife are Cuban. When his daughter Karina was having her coming out party, called *quince años* (fifteen years), Rosann and I went back to Miami for the celebration. It was a beautiful occasion, as elaborate as any wedding.

Jeff and his wife, Vicki, eventually moved to Chattanooga, Tennessee. We stayed friends with them for decades. Some years ago, I hired Jeff to run the parts and shipping department of an aviation-repair company I owned in Gadsden, Alabama. I was very hesitant to do so as I worried the friendship would suffer if the job failed. I was right to worry. My chief of maintenance was not happy that I hired someone else for the job, and he seemed to be always finding fault with Jeff. Eventually it was bad enough that I had to choose between my chief of maintenance and Jeff, so I had to let Jeff go. We've hardly spoken since, except for occasional Facebook posts. It can be hard on relationships when you have to put business first. Another of life's difficult lessons.

Jeff passed away two weeks before writing this. He was another lifetime smoker, did not exercise, and probably did not eat as healthily as he should have. He went into the hospital to have his colon removed, but his gut was full of a vile concoction that made him deathly ill. His body did not tolerate the anesthesia well and the doctors had to sedate him again. He never woke up. I am back in touch with Vicki and Jeff's two daughters, who still call me Uncle Rick. They have a difficult time ahead of them and I intend to be there for them.

CHAPTER 10

The Wild Blue Yonder

I graduated from the University of Miami with a Bachelor of Science in computer science and mathematics in May 1977. I received a reserve commission as a second lieutenant and a pilot slot in the United States Air Force but would have to wait six months before starting Undergraduate Pilot Training (UPT). I was fortunate to have retained my pilot slot as the USAF cut nine of thirteen pilot slots from my graduating ROTC class the summer before my senior year. I am certain my high GPA (3.6) was a deciding factor. My UPT assignment was changed twice until they finally decided I would go to Vance AFB in Enid, Oklahoma.

My wife and I were raised on Long Island, New York, not far from New York City. Enid, Oklahoma, was a very different kind of place. We found an apartment on the far west end of town. The view out our front window to the west was of pastureland as far as the eye could see, with lots of cows. Welcome to the heartland.

UPT was a challenging yearlong course of academics, along with T-37 and T-38 flying. This was only the beginning of learning to be a professional military pilot. We immersed ourselves in aircraft systems, weather, navigation, aerodynamics, aerobatics, instruments, and formation flying.

We worked twelve hours a day, five or six days a week. There was little time for socializing beyond Friday night at the officer's club on base. The key to success was time management and mission focus. We all knew our follow-on assignments would be predicated on our class ranking and whether we achieved a recommendation for fighters.

We had to solo each aircraft type in ten flights, which we call "sorties," or less. That was part of the pressure. During college the air force paid for twenty hours of flight training at a local flight school, and we had the same solo requirement. Obviously, the air force was already pushing to see who would excel under pressure.

My instructor (IP) during T-37 phase was Major David Thrames. David had flown the B-58 Hustler, a Cold War supersonic bomber, and had also been a commander at the USAF survival school in Spokane, Washington. To say he was a tough taskmaster is an understatement. I finally asked him one day if he could dial it back a little. He looked me straight in the eye and said, "No!" They must have thought me a very patient person, being able to flourish under David's demanding demeanor, because they decided to make me an IP.

I moved through T-37 phase into the T-38. It was like getting out of an old Chevy family car and being given a new Corvette to play with. What a great aircraft! Mach speed of 1.6; 720 degrees-per-second roll rate; 180 mph on final approach. This was our first taste of real high performance, and I couldn't get enough of it!

My wife was pregnant with our first child in the middle of the T-38 phase. Richard Patrick was born on August 25, 1978. My IP's wife was also due around the same time, so during the last month or so of their pregnancies, we'd look at each other and think, *if they call us back, will it be your wife or mine?*

I graduated UPT with my Fighter/Attack/Reconnaissance (FAR) recommendation, and they made me a First Assignment IP (FAIP) in T-37s. I was somewhat disappointed but decided to make the most of the assignment.

Richard Patrick (Rick) was born about three months before I graduated UPT. Rosann was great, covering all parenting duties on weekdays, and I would help on weekends. Rick was not an easy baby to care for. He had digestive problems and was a finicky eater. Rosann's mom, Josephine, was a godsend, coming out for regular visits to help take care of Rick. I remember her bouncing Rick on her knee while I entertained him with handstands against the wall of our apartment, trying to get him to eat.

We drove to Randolph AFB in San Antonio, Texas, for instructor training. It is a beautiful old base, and we really liked the big town. I learned to fly and teach from the right seat of the T-37 while looking cross-cockpit at the student's instruments. I particularly remember one formation sortie. I was on my leader's wing on our recovery as we flew formation through thick clouds. I concentrated completely on maintaining the correct position just three feet from his right wing tip. The problem was my inner ear began to sense we were in a ninety-degree bank. It took all my discipline to ignore what my head was telling me and just focus on my visual references on the lead's aircraft. When we finally broke out of the clouds we were in perfect straight-and-level flight. My head *caged* upright instantly, but that was a scary experience.

Rosann ended up going to the hospital during our stay in San Antonio. She had severe stomach pain that appeared to be appendicitis but turned out to be an inflamed pelvis from Rick's birth six months before. We learned the value of friends and family as my classmates and their wives took care of Rick until Josephine could fly in to help care for him. Throughout my air force and airline career, we had come to count on those closest to us to help in emergencies, and they counted on us. "Family" does not have to share blood!

We returned to Enid, Oklahoma, to start my IP tour in May 1979 and moved into base housing. I bought a bicycle and pedaled to the flight line every day, come rain or shine. We had some interesting IPs in the squadron. I was assigned to A Flight and spent three years teaching students to fly the T-37. Our students came from all over the world: Africa, the Middle East, Europe, and South America. My first student was a Dane named Bo K Rasmussen, nicknamed "BOK." Bo was probably one of the best pilots I ever trained. A natural, he made my job easy.

I also trained some pilots who would join me at Delta Air Lines many years later. It makes me smile to remember how I worried if a particular student was ready for his initial solo and then would see him decades later as a seasoned and confident airline captain. Good stuff indeed. I also made some lifelong friends among the IPs. Bill Barbour was a former F-4 pilot who was also an instructor in A Flight. A man's man, I liked Bill very much and continued to see him occasionally in Atlanta when we both lived there years later.

One fond memory I have from my time as an IP is a little humorous, but it also gives you an idea about the aggressive nature of military pilots. A handful of us IPs smoked back then. One of the students complained to the flight commander, so he pulled us offenders aside and told us, "You guys can't smoke cigarettes in the flight room anymore." No problem. We all showed up with cigars the next day. Needless to say, there were no more complaints about our cigarettes. Yes, it's harsh and wouldn't be tolerated today, but it does highlight the "take no prisoners" attitude shown by military pilots all over the world.

During my time with the squadron, in the very early '80s, we had the distinction of training the first female pilots in the USAF. It took that long for the military to learn that women could fly airplanes just as well as men. Unfortunately, not all the initial candidates belonged in UPT. We had one candidate who was a bit older, had waivers for her age along with some medical issues. Her instructors complained to our squadron management that she was not handling the training well and should be reviewed for continuing in UPT. There must have been great pressure to continue her training. Sadly, she crashed a T-37 during a solo flight while performing aerobatics. There was not a remaining piece of the aircraft bigger than a basketball. I flew the missing man formation at her funeral and met her family. It was a very sad event.

My first daughter, Christina Marie, was born while I was an IP in Oklahoma, just seventeen months after Rick. Rosann had traveled back home to New York as her time approached. The doctor said she could have the baby anytime, but please, "Not during my office hours!" Of course, that's exactly when Rosann went into labor. At four o'clock on the afternoon of January 28, 1980, we were in the labor room with Rosann saying, "I'm going to push!" and me replying, "No, you're not! Just keep breathing!" The doctor arrived just as she was being wheeled into the delivery room. By the time the anesthesiologist arrived, Christina Marie (Chrissy) was already born.

While in Oklahoma I had an opportunity to go to a detachment at a Strategic Air Command (SAC) base for a few months of flying with SAC copilots. I dropped off my family in New York, then I drove twelve hours to Loring AFB in Maine. It was the middle of the winter. The very next day I flew three times. On the third sortie of the day, the copilot and I forgot to lower the landing gear and ended up on our belly on the runway at sunset. The investigator told me that, at a critical time in the landing pattern, a radio transmission distracted us, causing us to make the error.

This was a devastating event for me. I was still a young lieutenant with what I hoped was a long career ahead of me and I had just damaged an aircraft. I sat in my room for days in the visiting officer's quarters (VOQ), chain smoking, wondering if I would ever be able to live down the infamy of this accident. After the investigation team was through, I returned to Oklahoma with my tail between my legs. From that moment on, I did everything I could to prove (including to myself) that I was not a screw up, that I could hold my own as a pilot against anyone. That was forty-five years ago, and I believe that event changed me forever as I am still a driven individual, trying to accomplish as much as I can every day.

I must have been successful because the squadron leadership

eventually let me go up to Wurtsmith AFB, Michigan, to fly with the SAC copilots stationed there. I had a successful tour and returned to earn an award as best instructor pilot. The prize was a trip in a T-38 to Eglin AFB in the Florida panhandle to fly the F-15 Eagle. What a jet! On takeoff, by the end of the runway, we were accelerating through 350 KIAS (Knots Indicated Airspeed) and stood the aircraft on its tail. Twelve thousand feet later I looked back through the double tail to see we were still climbing with the runway directly below!

We spent a week practicing many different missions in the F-15: training new wingmen, air-combat maneuvering, combat air patrol, and night intercepts. You have to be in the cockpit at night, in a screaming supersonic descent over a pitch-black ocean, to really appreciate the intensity and skill level of American fighter pilots. I returned to Oklahoma a very motivated IP.

I also started an MBA program at Phillips University while based in Enid. My days were spent on the flight line and my nights at the school, with a little time on weekends for family. Again, I have to give Rosann a lot of credit for covering for me, her driven husband. I graduated with a perfect 4.0 average in just eighteen months. I wasn't sure how I might make use of this new degree, but it was an important accomplishment that swelled my sense of self-worth.

By now I wanted to fly fighters, but the assignment board for instructors tried to spread the wealth of our experience to all the other major commands. I was assigned to fly the C-141 Starlifter at McGuire AFB in New Jersey. That was a plum assignment for "heavies" and was close to our families in New York. My positives had earned me a good assignment, but the incident in Maine had an impact too. That was okay. I was ready to join an operational unit and see the world!

CHAPTER 11

Blue Diamond

Rosann and I left Enid in February 1982 for Altus, Oklahoma, where I would learn to fly the C-141. We had two very young kids in tow and found the small town pleasant, but it was extremely difficult to find adequate housing. After a few frustrating days looking, we decided to send Rosann and the kids back to New York to stay with her parents while I completed the three-month school in Altus.

The C-141 is long since retired but I look back on it with great affection. It was a very large, complicated aircraft that handled very well and was quite dependable. At 325,000 pounds maximum takeoff weight and a wingspan of 160 feet, plus two of every kind of instrument, radio, and navigation equipment, I was initially overwhelmed with learning to manage all this information. One of my instructors would stuff a wad of dip in his mouth before a four-hour training sortie and not spit the entire time! What a guy!

I finished copilot school in May 1982 and drove out of the base on my way to rejoin my family in New York. I heard a tornado damaged the base a week after I left. Talk about timing. I drove to Long Island to reunite with my family before going house hunting in central New Jersey.

When I got home, I learned Rosann was having some trouble getting along with her sister Marie's husband, Doug. Doug is an interesting guy. He is an auto mechanic by trade, came very close to completing a bachelor's degree, and could have opened his own shop at any time. It is fascinating to see how sometimes people hold themselves back from accomplishing more.

Anyway, Doug and Rosann grated on each other, so I went to his workshop to have a talk with him. He yelled and I talked. Afterward he shook my hand and thanked me. I think Doug understood I was trying to put family first. My difficult upbringing made me want to fix what was wrong rather than make matters worse.

I contacted a realtor and in short order we found a big house in Willingboro, New Jersey, about thirty minutes from the base. An elderly widow lived there alone, and we came to an agreement without much fuss. The biggest worry at the time was the interest rate. Jimmy Carter was president and mortgage rates were in the 15–16 percent range. On an air force captain's salary, the high interest rate really limited how much house you could buy.

Over a two-and-a-half-year period we did a lot of upgrades to the house, most of which I did myself: alarm system, new flooring, inside and outside paint, etc. This was our first house, and we worked hard to make it our home. We also traveled back and forth to New York to see family as often as possible. After the years of being away in college and my initial tour in the air force, it was fun watching our children enjoy the warmth of a close extended family.

I quickly settled into squadron life at the 18th Military Airlift Squadron (MAS). Our squadron patch was a blue diamond, and the joke was that a girl's best friend was a blue diamond. We flew everywhere: Europe, Africa, the Middle East, North and South America, Asia. We also participated in just about every conflict or relief effort during that period, and our squadron even brought the dead followers and victims of Reverend Jim Jones home from Guyana. We supported Chad in North Africa when Gaddafi was stirring up trouble. We airlifted

Special Forces in and out of Central America when the Sandinistas controlled Nicaragua. You would be amazed how hard it is to keep your eyes open after a twenty-four-hour workday of shuttling troops back and forth to an operational area.

As a brand-new aircraft commander (AC), I was excited to be a part of the Grenada island invasion in 1983. We were placed on alert status, then moved into on-base quarters, and finally flew to a staging area and briefed on the operation. We were not allowed to operate the aircraft at war weights, so our fuel load was limited. We were basically told to fly south, offload our troops and their equipment at the former Point Salines airfield, and then fly as far north as we could before stopping for fuel. I did this multiple times and always managed to make it back to the staging area in North Carolina, but it was a very challenging operation. The Cuban embassy on the island was monitoring our radio transmissions and coordinated shelling of the airport as aircraft were on final.

On the first night, we set up a twelve-mile final approach using our inertial navigation system (INS) and then flew a blacked-out approach using the weather radar to "paint" the peninsula where the airport was located. We flew in from over the water at just a few hundred feet during a rainstorm, saw the smudge pots along the runway edge, and turned on the landing lights at fifty feet above the surface. As soon as we touched down, we turned the landing lights off again. At the end of the runway, we turned around, set the parking brake, placed all four engines in reverse, opened the rear cargo doors, and disgorged the troops and equipment. Then it was a controlled dash to close the doors, tie down any remaining cargo, and take off back the way we landed.

On that first mission the troop commander did not have very good intelligence on what to expect. Only by coincidence my wife and I had been on the island as tourists just a few months before. I spent half the southern-heading flight briefing the commander on everything I could remember from our week on Grenada. I proudly earned my first Air Medal for that operation.

On one of these missions my copilot was a devout Mormon. His eyes got as big as saucers as he listened to marine combat helicopters duking it out with the Cuban troops. We also brought home some of the aircrew who were shot down. Their bodies were stuck in the wreckage for a few days, decaying in the sweltering tropical heat. Even though they were tightly enclosed in body bags and coffins, the smell was horrific. It was a sickly-sweet smell that could never be mistaken for anything else. Another lesson was being brought home with me: This job was for real, and sometimes for keeps.

On one of my later missions into Grenada, I flew as an "adviser" with an all-women crew, making them the first women to fly into a combat zone. That certainly made headlines. Then after the conflict was over, we flew fifty-thousand-pound loads of Soviet armament to Washington, DC, so the world could learn how the Russians were planning to cause trouble throughout Latin America.

Later that fall of 1983 we had the sad task of bringing home the bodies from the barracks bombing in Beirut, Lebanon, and dropping off the fresh-faced marine replacements. There were so many bodies—241 marines, sailors, and soldiers. Again, the sobering reminder was that the world was a dangerous place, and we were constantly sent to the heart of its conflicts!

———

Not all the situations we found ourselves in were dangerous. In fact, some of them were downright humorous. I remember an exercise where an oversized, wheeled army vehicle was brought out to a C-141 to be loaded. The command post later called out to the airplane to say, according to their calculations, that the vehicle was too large for the Starlifter's cargo compartment. "Don't try to load it!"

The loadmaster's response was: "So, you want me to take it off the airplane now?"

One of the missions we often flew was called the 7Papa3 run. We would fly to Rota, Spain, and Sigonella, Italy, pull an all-nighter down to Nairobi, Kenya, and spend two weeks supporting the US Navy at Diego Garcia in the Indian Ocean. One night the crew decided to go to a nightclub in Nairobi called the New Florida Club. One of my flight engineers had met a local girl and spent the evening drinking and dancing with her. At the end of the night, he told me he just wanted to go back to the hotel, but the girl insisted he go back to her village with her. I snuck him out and into a taxi, but she chased us outside and caused a scene.

There we were, two White boys, on an East African city street at two in the morning, surrounded by a crowd and confronted by an angry woman. How did I get into this mess? I finally appealed to the nearest bystander and beseeched him to help get this girl off our back. He grabbed her arms and we jumped in the taxi. The engineer was so appreciative of my help that he paid the taxi fare. Of course, we found out the next day the driver had charged us four times the going rate!

On another trip we ended up in Oklahoma City for the night. The hotel bar had a three-for-one happy hour. Oh boy, this was going to be an interesting night. We went next door after happy hour to a country-and-western place called Cow Daddy's. You can see this coming a mile away, right?

My aircraft commander, a crusty old major, slipped away from our table to talk to a couple of girls who had sat down at the table behind ours. I looked over and saw that he had a hand on one of the girl's thighs. I also saw a bouncer hustling over with evil intent in his eye. I quickly got up, dragged the major to his feet, and looked that bouncer straight in the eyes, saying, "Just help me get him to the door." I put that fellow to bed to sleep off the booze, but I don't think he ever knew how close he came to getting the cow patty kicked out of him!

During 1983 I kept track of my missions away from base. That year I spent about 240 days deployed. That is two out of every three days. I learned this was not easy on me, nor on my family. Rosann finally confided to me that she was tempted to start drinking and was reading the Bible every day to get through being left alone so much. I was scared for her and the children, and worried my career was destroying my marriage. The two kids were only four and six years old. They depended on her for everything. Heck, *I* depended on her for everything at home. Rosann finally landed a part-time job as a nurse, and that seemed to help her feel a bit less isolated.

I was still worried about my family and the stress on my wife. I was leaving her alone a lot and the combat-support deployments made her worry about losing me. I decided to investigate my options. One of Rosann's older cousins had a connection with the flight department of a large New York company and offered to help me get a flying job there if I wanted to leave the air force. I also had an offer to join the Secret Service after helping deploy President Reagan's entourage of agents and support equipment during a China visit. While both offers were tempting, the reality was I would be gone from home just as much as I currently was. For the sake of family, I had to politely decline both offers.

The air force was just standing up Space Command in Colorado Springs at that time. I researched getting a master's degree in space technology and switching career fields. Finally, a call went out for qualified candidates to apply to NASA for the Space Shuttle program as mission specialists. I met all the astronaut qualifications but, again, there would be a lot of time away from family, and I was trying to find a solution that kept me home more rather than less. As selfishly hard-charging as we pilots could be, an important part of me was screaming to give the family the priority it so sorely deserved.

A bit of a last resort finally offered itself to me in the opening of instructor pilot positions in a new Air Training Command (ATC) program at Sheppard AFB in Wichita Falls, Texas. The Euro-NATO

Joint Jet Pilot Training (ENJJPT) program had been developed out of the old German Air Force (GAF) program at Sheppard. The idea was to provide a standard program of training for future fighter pilots. Both the students and the instructors would be from all the NATO countries. I applied for and was accepted for a T-38 Talon IP position.

I was very excited. I would be flying a high-performance, supersonic trainer and teaching future fighter pilots. The other instructors were almost exclusively experienced fighter pilots from every NATO country. Imagine all the things I could learn from these guys! But first I needed to sell a house.

I called the realtor who sold us our house in New Jersey, and we quickly had a buyer from New York. The buyer paid a hefty cash down payment and insisted we move out immediately. The air force packed up all our household goods, Rosann and the kids went to New York to stay with family again, and I moved in with a bachelor buddy. But it turned out the sale wasn't going to be easy. The buyer backed out of the deal at the last minute. He simply did not show up for closing. Seems he was scheduled to get married, but his wedding was canceled. We did end up selling the house shortly before moving to Texas, and I ended up keeping the deposit, which paid the additional expenses of the canceled closing.

Goodbye, New Jersey. Texas, here we come!

CHAPTER 12

ENJJPT

Rosann and I moved with our two young children and our Irish setter, Brandy, to Sheppard AFB in Wichita Falls, Texas, in April 1984. We found a house for rent very near the base. The backyard had an above-ground pool and a mile-long view of open mesquite fields. It reminded me of Enid, Oklahoma. The best part of this tour was going home every night to my family!

I processed into the squadron and was set up for a three-month indoctrination on flying the T-38 from the back seat and being an instructor pilot again. The T-38 was a wonderful aircraft—fast and maneuverable—and the students were all being prepared for follow-on assignments to fighter aircraft throughout NATO. The IP corps had a remarkably varied background: Danes had flown F-16s and Drakens; Norwegians F-16s and F-104s; Germans F-4s, Alpha Jets, and Tornadoes; and so on. I really enjoyed learning to teach tactical formation, low-level flying, and all the other components of advanced military flight training.

The kids settled into preschool, and we soon found out Rosann was pregnant again. We wanted four children, but this third pregnancy was difficult. Rosann went into early labor, and she ended up either in the hospital or bedridden for her last three to four months of pregnancy.

Even with twelve-hour workdays and six days a week on the flight line, I played Mr. Mom as best I could so Rosann could rest. It was a terribly grinding schedule: wake up early, get the kids ready for school, go to work, come home, feed them, do laundry, go to bed, and get up the next day to do it all again. I told people I would not wish single parenthood on even my worst enemies.

Diana was born on February 14, 1985, Valentine's Day. The birth was totally natural, and that made our family three for three on births I was present for! Diana smiled and laughed shortly after being brought home. We knew from the beginning she would be a special child.

Let me share a funny story from when we first moved into the Texas house. Rosann let the dog out into the fenced backyard one morning and it immediately started circling and barking up a storm. I was already at work, but a neighbor across the street heard the commotion and ran over with a garden hoe. He found the dog circling a snake that was longer than the hoe itself. So, he threw the hoe to the ground, ran home, and came back with a pistol! When I got home that night Rosann laughed hysterically as she described our neighbor firing away with his pistol while the dog continued circling and barking. The snake just slithered toward the back fence and into my wood pile. Snake: 1, Neighbor: 0.

The flying was great. The T-38 had pretty good range, and you could two-hop to either coast. We did weekend cross countries to Los Angeles, San Francisco, New York, and Florida. The students were generally a great bunch. They had made it through the T-37 phase and were confidently moving their way through to graduation and a fighter assignment.

The base itself was also a lot of fun. The officer's club was a popular place, especially the casual bar. All medical-service officers (doctors, dentists, and nurses) were initially trained at Sheppard AFB. These MIMSOs kept the bar hopping on Friday nights, as did all the foreign pilots. Every Friday afternoon, my German air force friend,

Rudi Dullein, would casually saunter up and say, "So, Richie Boy, we go to the club un have a sociable one, *ja*?" Of course one became two, became three, and so on. I tried for the first three months to keep up with the Europeans and then gave it up. There was no way to match their drinking prowess.

After a little more than a year as a T-38 IP I started guest flying with the Pilot Instructor Training (PIT) flight. I really enjoyed the challenge and difficulties of teaching other NATO instructor pilots. Imagine a foreign major or lieutenant colonel who had just finished a staff tour, hadn't flown fighters in three to five years, was not originally trained in the US system, and had a limited knowledge of English. And now it was our job to polish their English, train them to be instructors (maybe for the first time) in our American system, and teach them to fly from the back seat of an unfamiliar supersonic fighter/trainer aircraft. Oh yeah, and you only have three months to accomplish it all. It was a *very* rewarding experience and my favorite tour in the air force.

In 1985 the major airlines started to hire again after a long hiatus. I also had my sights set on a fighter assignment after my three-year tour at Sheppard ended. I began doing research and talking to everyone I could find about the airlines, Air National Guard (ANG), and Air Force Reserve flying units.

During one weekend cross country to San Antonio, I happened to be in the casual bar of the officer's club at Randolph AFB. They were hosting a reunion of Raven FACs, the secret CIA outfit based in Laos during the Vietnam War. A guy walked into the bar dressed in jeans, a T-shirt, and a long-haired hippie wig with an elephant's trunk hanging out of his pants zipper. A girl at the bar turned around, put one hand on the guy's shoulder and the other on the trunk, and said, "Damn glad to meet you!"

I thought, *Damn, I'm partying with those guys tonight!*

They were a fun bunch. I remember one guy, "Growth" Wilson, was as bald as a cue ball. Perfect nickname! I met another guy who was a captain for Delta Air Lines. He gave me his card and offered to give me a recommendation. But the next morning I thought about that. I asked myself: *Do I really want a recommendation from such a crazy dude?* Some years later he was killed in a T-6 Texan crash on a beach in the Florida panhandle after his engine failed. Unfortunately, his passenger, the brother of another Delta pilot, was also killed.

I started to contact ANG and reserve units about joining them while continuing to make plans to apply to the airlines. Another funny story, one of our fellow IPs was getting ready to apply to the airlines as well. All of them required 20/20 vision. This fellow had slightly weak eyes, but the doctor told him if he put an eye exercise chart on the wall and focused on it every day, he could improve his vision. Well, when he went out to fly each day, we would take that chart to a copy machine and shrink it just a few percent. After a week he was really sweating, thinking his eyesight was suddenly deteriorating. We finally let him in on the joke. To his credit, he took our ribbing in good spirits.

Rosann and I had some fun with our time in Texas. It was hard to get her to go out on a Friday or Saturday night, but the base had a good day care center, and we tried to get out a couple of times each month. We would travel back to New York for vacations, where she, Marie, and their mom would traipse around New York, as always, like the Three Musketeers. I would look up old friends or go fishing with Rosann's dad, Prosper.

I started Rick and myself in a martial arts class on base when he was five. It was excellent exercise and training, and a great confidence builder for Rick. A bully picked on him one day and Rick stopped just short of breaking the kid's arm. They became friends after that. I was glad Rick had that experience. I competed in some local and regional tournaments and won a couple of minor trophies. I liked the training enough to continue it for ten more years, even when we moved to Atlanta, Georgia.

My kid brother Raymond is ten years younger than me and enlisted in the air force right out of high school. Raymond had a fascination with bugs and became an entomology expert in the civil engineering department. During our time in Wichita Falls, he was stationed at Carswell AFB in Fort Worth, Texas, just a few hours away. We would alternate visiting each other on many weekends.

Raymond married his high school sweetheart. She was very dedicated to Raymond and their two children, but she was also a bit of a drill sergeant. She made no bones about who ruled the roost. When we would visit, we were careful to do exactly what she wanted, on the schedule she set, or else there would be fireworks. One morning while visiting, Rosann made an early breakfast for our kids since they were so young, and they were hungry. When Raymond's wife got up, she lit into us with curses because she had been planning a big breakfast. That drove a wedge between the families that took a long time to heal.

Raymond's wife later had a few miscarriages, and she was having a hard time. I confronted our other brother, Tim, who was being a hard-ass and less than sympathetic, on her behalf. I really appreciated when she later admitted to me that she was sometimes difficult to get along with, and that she appreciated what I did in her defense. As I got older, I wanted better relationships with my extended family, but I was also learning, as Mick Jagger sang, you don't always get what you want.

Back at the flying squadron, I was planning my shotgun approach for getting hired by the airlines and an ANG unit. The idea of a part-time military gig and a full-time airline job seemed the best of both worlds. I even had an unsolicited offer to join other government agencies as a pilot. With the airlines hiring, experienced professional pilots had many opportunities. I also figured that ANG and reserve units would be hiring too, as many of their pilots left for the airlines and either quit flying for their guard unit or retired from them.

About halfway through my tour, I was offered the chief of academics position. I dived into the responsibilities and enjoyed the work. We taught everything those young student pilots would need to go on and fly fighters: systems, instruments, low-level planning, formation, aerodynamics, weather, and numerous other subjects. I had a chance to brief in-depth subjects to all levels within the wing and was even selected to join the standardization/evaluation section until I announced my decision to leave active duty. Interesting, because I also had a fitness report soon to be signed by a general officer, but the report was "pulled" from his desk at the last minute. Leaving active duty was like being a traitor. Did they not see that I was continuing my career, and would do so for another fifteen years?

I applied to and was accepted by several fighter ANG units. I had an offer to fly the reconnaissance-mission RF-4 in Louisville, and two offers to fly the A-10 Warthog in New England. It was not an easy decision. "Kill 'em with film" or blow things up. In the end I chose the A-10 ANG unit out of Westfield, Massachusetts, and in April of 1987 I left active duty and reported to my new unit.

Before I could report to Massachusetts, I would need to learn how to fly the jet. I was hoping to go through the full fighter pilot lead-in program at Holloman AFB in New Mexico, but they didn't have a slot for my time frame, so I left Texas and reported directly to the reserve training unit at Barksdale AFB in Bossier City, Louisiana. As an ENJJPT T-38 IP, I felt very ready to fly the A-10.

There were no rooms available in the busy on-base visiting officer's quarters, so most of my class was sent to a local motel. It was close by and clean enough, but it was not the Hilton by any means. I remember one Sunday afternoon when a commotion caused many of us to step outside. Two local men and a woman were having a knock-down, drag-out fight that ended with one fellow chasing the other two with a length of pipe. Katie, bar the door!

Bossier City and Shreveport were neat places though, right on the Red River. We all looked forward to some local eating and drinking places on Friday and Saturday nights. The Superior Bar and Grill on the south side of Shreveport had a happy hour that featured frozen margaritas from a soft-serve ice cream machine.

I really liked flying the A-10 Warthog. It's a big straight-wing aircraft with an incredible ability to place weapons on target. We used a procedural trainer to review all normal and emergency checklists, then went out to the flight line to do an engine start with our instructor standing on the left side ladder watching us. The next time we walked out to the airplane it was for a solo flight, our IP in another aircraft on our wing. This was how they did things in WWII, and it was so much fun to be cut loose in this beast!

The training was straightforward: visual and pattern work, formation, and instrument approaches. The best part was learning to drop bombs and shoot the gun, as well as learning how to apply tactics in a low- or high-threat environment. On one sortie, we flew to the Razorback Range in Arkansas. I was leading my instructor on a low-altitude bombing run, using terrain to mask our approach to the target. My wingman said, "Rich, did you see that?"

I had been focused on our approach to the target, so I said, "No, what was it?"

He replied, "That ultralight that just passed between us!" Even on a military bombing range you absolutely needed to keep your head on a swivel.

Rosann and the kids finally finished up the school year and joined me for the last half of my training. One of the KC-10 pilots I knew was away for a few months, so I arranged to sublet his apartment. It was good to have the family back together, but in short order I completed my training, and we once again packed up for the move to Massachusetts. I sent Rosann, Chrissy, and Diana ahead by airline, and Rick and I drove to Massachusetts. It was a neat experience having my young son on the road with me for a couple of days. Just a little male bonding.

Applying for the airlines proved to be an interesting and, ultimately, more difficult endeavor than I had anticipated. I had traveled down to Brownsville, Texas, while I was a T-38 IP, for a flight school that issued Airline Transport Pilot (ATP) licenses. I also had to take several written FAA tests for the ATP and dispatcher licenses. I wanted to be ready for anything.

I did the first interview with American Airlines in Dallas. They sent me a rejection letter shortly after the interview. I asked myself, "What could have possibly gone wrong?" I had a physical while in Dallas to include blood work. So, I went to my air force flight surgeon, and he ran the tests himself. That's when I found out I had high cholesterol. It's a family trait, and I'm sure our typical Western diet wasn't helping. Since passing the FAA Class 1 physical is a pretty demanding event, and required every six months, it made sense that the airlines were very strict about a candidate's health during the hiring process. I immediately made severe changes to my diet: whole grains and fruit for breakfast, salad for lunch, and a very healthy dinner of fish or chicken with vegetables.

The diet changes, coupled with an aggressive exercise routine, must have worked. I reapplied to American and was invited back. Mission accomplished. But high cholesterol and its negative effects on my coronary system would come back to haunt me much later in life.

I also interviewed with the Flying Tigers in Los Angeles. The interview went well. I flew the B-747 simulator, and they offered me a position starting immediately. Unfortunately, I was just starting school for the A-10, and their offer was withdrawn when I could not start right away.

Then I traveled to Pittsburgh to interview with USAir. I flew their DC-9 simulator and was put in the left seat and set up for a precision ILS approach. I flew the aircraft well, and afterward the captain instructor told me, "You could have turned on the flight director."

I responded, "I would have if you had shown me how to turn

it on." They gave me a class date, but I put them off one additional month while I finished A-10 training.

In that intervening month, I had not yet heard from Delta Air Lines, so I called their hiring department. The girl said, "Your application is on my desk, and I was just about to call you." The problem was I had moved from my last address in Texas, and both my address and phone number had changed. Truly, the good Lord was looking out for me.

The interview went well. Of course, most pilot applicants showed up with dark suits and red "power" ties, because that was the rumored preferred attire. I showed up in a light gray suit with a blue tie, because that was what I owned.

There were three interviews, one each with an administrator, a chief pilot, and a retired captain. The admin guy was no problem, and the chief pilot was very nice, telling me he saw no reason why I shouldn't be hired. I later found out he said that to everyone.

The retired captain interview was another situation altogether. He came out of his small office holding a folder and said, "Hess, Richard Hess." I jumped up like a jack-in-the-box. He had a very serious demeanor and said, "Good morning. I'm Captain Charles so-and-so." His last name escapes me now almost forty years later.

I stuck out my hand and said, "Good morning, Chuck. Glad to meet you." My fellow applicants just shook their heads and thought, *That's it. Hess is toast!*

The captain asked me some strange questions like, "Where would you be if you were at zero degrees latitude and longitude?" The whole time it seemed like he was trying to get a rise out of me. I just kept calmly answering his questions. Finally, he asked if I had applied to any other airlines. I told him yes, but I considered Delta my number one choice and wanted to fly for them if possible.

I traveled back to Barksdale AFB in Louisiana where I was finishing A-10 school with the reserves. Four days later Delta called and offered me a job. My shout of joy could be heard in Texas! I was very pleased with myself. Some of the other airlines I applied with either went out of business or were merged over the last forty years, but Delta would prove to be the best, most stable place for me over the following three decades.

Thank you, Delta Air Lines!

CHAPTER 13

The Warthog

Before I dive too deep into my airline experience, I would like to reminisce a bit about flying the A-10 those three years, from 1987 to 1990. It may not be as fast as a T-38 or an F-15, but the air-to-ground mission sure made it a lot of fun to fly. This was a purpose-built aircraft, its primary mission to destroy enemy armor.

The A-10 carries 1,174 rounds of 30mm ammunition in the GAU 8/A Avenger rotary cannon. Its seven barrels spit out 4,200 rounds per minute. That's seventy rounds per second. On a hot, humid summer day you can actually see the bullets going supersonic. I remember the very first time I shot the cannon. It growls at you and shakes the heads-up display enough to blur the imagery. Then you smell the burnt powder through the air-conditioning system. I remember a huge feeling of excitement at being able to release such power with a single squeeze of the trigger.

The A-10 Warthog also carries an amazing array of rockets, missiles, and bombs. We practiced regularly with 70mm and 127mm rockets, TV- and infrared-guided AGM-65 Maverick missiles, parachute, and fin-retarded bombs, as well as cluster munitions and the Mark series of 500-, 750-, and 2,000-pound unguided bombs. When I flew the aircraft in the late 1980s the USAF had not yet upgraded the Warthog to carry "smart weapons" such as the JDAM and wind-corrected munitions. Every bombing mission had a range officer scoring the accuracy of your delivery. We got pretty darn good to the point that, after an entire year, some of us had an average bomb score of half a wingspan!

In three years, I amassed 550 hours flying the A-10. That's not bad considering it was a part-time job that competed with the airline and family for my time. We were very busy as a unit, doing several interesting deployments in the US and Europe.

I also flew a number of these jets out to McClellan AFB in Sacramento, California, where the A-10 went through depot-level maintenance. The best leg of that trip was approaching Hill AFB in Ogden, Utah. I would cancel my instrument flight plan about a hundred miles east of Hill and drop down to fly low-level across the high plateau leading to the Wasatch Range. I would then pop up, contact Hill, and do a visual arrival. Great fun!

Our guard unit did a few deployments out West during my three years. We would go to George AFB in Victorville, California, and act as the "red air"—bad guys—for the army units doing their desert exercises at the Fort Irwin National Training Center in California. They fitted laser designators to our aircraft and laser receivers to the army vehicles. If we put enough energy into the receiver, that vehicle would light up with flashing red lights and be considered "destroyed."

I remember to this day skimming head-height across dry lake beds at four hundred miles per hour in tactical formation and popping up to attack the army vehicles in the valley beyond landmarks the army named "Chinaman's Hat" (which, looking back, we wouldn't use today) and "John Wayne Pass." We "killed" a lot of vehicles. I also remember being in bed, dead asleep, when the bed started rocking like a giant hand was shaking it. That was my first earthquake, and it was an unsettling experience.

We also deployed to Davis-Monthan AFB in Tucson during one winter for a "snowbird" exercise. I enjoyed the wide-open desert ranges of southern Arizona. There happened to be an air force annual crud tournament going on while we were there in the officer's club. Crud is a contact sport played on a pool table. The Royal Canadian Air Force invented the sport, and it became popular with many military units. None of my guard buddies wanted to play, so I ended up with a marine helicopter crew. We lost in the early rounds, but it didn't matter. Great fun was had by all.

The Cold War was still hot during the late 1980s. Our guard unit had a wartime location in Yenişehir, Turkey, on the south coast of the Sea of Marmara. We lived in tents by the side of the runway, ate MREs (meals ready to eat) like army grunts, and showered in a tiny, unheated block building. The hot-water tank was also tiny, and suffice it to say, by the time I, a lowly captain, took my shower, there was no hot water remaining. Our toilet was a porcelain hole in the floor. One of our more creative fellows knocked the bottom out of a chair and nailed a toilet seat to it. Bullseye! At night or in the early morning you would feel snails crunching under your boots because they climbed the stalks of grass. Strange place.

You could not complain about the flying though. I often had the early morning missions. Up at 0400, fed and briefed by 0500, and airborne by 0600. As soon as we cleared the runway and got the landing gear up, the leader would point you out to tactical spread, which happened to be right over our tent city. Hey, if we had to be up early, why shouldn't the rest of the gang?

We would fly west along the seacoast to Eskişehir and "jump" the Turkish F-5 fighters as they took off from the runway until the Turkish controller yelled at us to "go away!" Then, while crossing the Sea of Marmara on our way to the Eastern Thrace, it was not uncommon to encounter a Russian ship or submarine transiting between the Mediterranean and Black Seas. So, of course, we would "circle the wagons" over the ship and make a general nuisance of ourselves, then continue to the Thrace.

One morning we came over a hill on the Thrace at about fifty feet and three hundred knots, and there in front of me was a shepherd with a sizable herd of sheep. Those sheep scattered at the first sound of our engines screaming over their heads, and the shepherd waved his staff furiously in the air as we safely slipped over the next ridgeline.

Next, we might move on to the mountains in the far west of Turkey bordering with Bulgaria, flying just high enough along the border to let them know we were there. As I said, it was the Cold War, and military units on both sides exhibited aggressive behavior toward the other. Looking back, it seems we were young and foolish and had more than enough testosterone to cloud our judgment. It just seemed important to let those on the other side of the Iron Curtain know we did not fear them, and we were ready for whatever they might throw at us.

During our Turkey deployment we were instructed to act again as the "red air" for a joint US-Turkish amphibious marine exercise. As the troops came ashore, we rolled in two by two to attack them. Suddenly a Smokey SAM rose into the sky. The US used what looked like very large bottle rockets to simulate a surface-to-air missile launch. I remember we took evasive action and dropped down behind a ridgeline. My leader asked me if I knew where the Smokey SAM had been launched from. I immediately responded, "Yes. You attack the troops. I'll take care of the SAM."

He then rolled over the ridge to continue his attack while I broke off to find the threat. I could see the guy who was launching the SAMs standing in a big open field. I was flying so low that I literally had to knife-edge to pass between two trees. The last thing I saw of this guy before I flew low over his head and blasted him with my engine exhaust was him trying to run away from me while looking back over his shoulder. There were no more Smokey SAMs launched that day.

I flew one of the A-10s home to Massachusetts, and we overnighted at Lajes Field in the Azores. On the deployment to Turkey, I remember what a pain it was getting out of all the thermal and survival clothing—and then trying to get your privates into a plastic bag just to pee. You usually ended up making a mess of yourself. So, for the last eight-hour flight home, I promised myself I would not pee for the entire flight. I managed to keep my promise, but my God was I hurting the last two hours. As soon as I shut down the aircraft and dismounted, I rushed over to the grass at the edge of the ramp and watered the lawn, as did most of the other pilots.

My last deployment was to a Red Flag exercise at Nellis AFB, Nevada, in the spring of 1990. This was an amazing place, with every kind of fighter aircraft imaginable present. We were briefed on the exercise and the different ranges: live-fire, electronic, air-to-air, and the infamous Area 51. And we were warned: any intrusion into Area 51 would get us instantly grounded and sent home.

We would usually arrive early, brief the mission, then take off and fly a very large counterclockwise route, first to a rendezvous with an air refueling tanker, then dropping down into the air-to-air range where F-16s were waiting to jump us. Then it was across the electronic warfare range and finally the live-fire range where we could drop our bombs. The return routing to Nellis took us across Yucca Flat, where all the below-ground nuclear testing was conducted. It was a very strange sight to see an incredible number of large circular depressions, each one caused by the detonation of an individual nuclear device.

One of my last flights on the range was with my squadron commander. He and I did not get along very well, but I led the mission, and he didn't have much to say in the debriefing. Soon after, I planned and led the redeployment of ten A-10s from Nevada back to our home base in Massachusetts. It was a gratifying end to our deployment with an air refueling along the way.

The next time I was at the unit the squadron commander asked to see me. We had a long talk, and the basic gist was that he didn't think I fit in very well and that I should consider leaving for another unit. He was right; it just didn't make it any easier hearing it from him.

I had proved I was a capable pilot. In fact, I was the best bomber in the squadron for that whole year, according to the bomb scores. It was the aggressive atmosphere that just did not sit well with me. I think I knew this was coming, because a couple of months before I confided to a fellow squadron pilot that I had started talking to other guard units. I was already looking for a new home.

Once my unit's leadership knew this, they were only too happy to push me out and make room for the next pilot. That may seem harsh, but it made perfect sense. I wasn't happy in an extremely aggressive unit, where even physical confrontations were common. I had proven my ability to fly the aircraft and accomplish the mission, but I needed to find a better fit for me.

CHAPTER 14

Delta Air Lines

Those years were busy, flying the A-10 and for Delta Air Lines at the same time. I was hired at Delta on July 24, 1987, the same year I started flying the A-10, right in the middle of Delta's merge with Western Airlines. We had a class of twenty-four pilots, about half former navy, half former air force, and one marine. Our seniority ranking was based on our age, and I was exactly in the middle.

Rosann and the kids were just getting settled into the house in Massachusetts at that time, so I got together with some of my new classmates and rented an apartment near the Atlanta airport. The weird thing was that Rosann's father passed away the very day I got hired. I was torn between getting this important career started and being in New York for Pop's funeral. I decided to stay in Atlanta, and to this day question whether I made the right decision.

The other thing that has always bothered me is why Prosper died on the very day I started my new career. I've told many friends it feels spooky, wondering if Pop made a special deal with God so I could have this great opportunity. I know that sounds silly, but the next thirty-one years at Delta were really good compared to many other airlines that failed, went into bankruptcy, or endured difficult mergers.

Pop, I think of you often and hope you didn't give anything up for me. I thank God you were there for all of us through the early years.

Most of the first week of training was spent learning the Delta system and procedures, receiving briefings from people in various departments to include personnel, finance, operations, flight planning, and training. A Delta captain gave us a briefing on our finances. I remember his sage words, saying, "The best financial advice I can give you is to keep your first wife." However, the biggest thing that stuck with me that week was the incredibly rosy picture everyone was painting for us. I couldn't help but think of that Timbuk3 song, "The Future's So Bright, I Gotta Wear Shades"!

I would fly as a flight engineer for the first year at Delta. The initial training was very intense. Our systems instructors were all experienced former maintenance technicians. We learned the aircraft in great depth. In fact, before they would allow us to sit for our oral exam with the FAA, we had to draw every major system diagram from scratch on a blank sheet of paper. This included hydraulics, electrical, pressurization and air-conditioning, engines, APU, fire and overheat, braking, flight controls, and cockpit controls. It was rigorous, and I enjoyed the total immersion immensely.

Once we passed the FAA oral exam, which lasted for two to three hours, it was time to move on to simulator training. Since Delta had just merged with Western Airlines, their training facility in Los Angeles was made available to us on a volunteer basis. My simulator partner, Steve, and I decided to accept that offer and were on our way to LAX.

The sim training in Los Angeles was even more intense than the ground school in Atlanta. Our sim instructor was a retired C-141 Starlifter instructor engineer from the air force. I called each sim session "dial-a-disaster." He would give us some major system failure and hammer us to follow the memorized and written emergency procedures, then as soon as you put your manuals away and caught your breath, he would throw the next emergency at you. We were certainly ready for anything once we finished the simulator phase.

Of course, we had to take another FAA check ride in the sim before we would be allowed out "on the line." Our check airman was a former Western guy and an FAA designee. I remember him complaining about the seniority-list integration of the two airlines during a break. We were on probation for the first year, and it was probably stupid on my part, but I told him, "I don't know why you're complaining. Western was not doing well and now you have a very bright future ahead with Delta." He just looked at me funny and didn't say a word. We completed the check rides, and Steve and I hopped an all-nighter back to Atlanta.

That all-nighter was one to remember. It was an L-1011 aircraft and of course I had the middle seat in the very back. The Lockheed TriStar had a coach seating arrangement of five middle seats and two seats on either side by the windows. I walked back to my row, checked my ticket, and looked at the seats. There were four large ladies, shoulder to shoulder, who filled the space. I looked at them, they looked at me, then they looked at each other. Finally, the two middle ladies leaned apart, and there was my seat buried between them. To say that was an uncomfortable four-hour flight home is an understatement, especially when one of those nice ladies fell asleep on my shoulder!

My first assignment after training was to the Miami/Fort Lauderdale pilot base. It would mean more time away from home, but I would be able to bid up to the Boston base in a few months. In the meantime, I rented a room in one of our scheduler's homes, and that turned out to be fortuitous. Each pilot's schedule was individually built by the local schedulers at that time. John, the guy who rented me the room, did a great job of manipulating my schedule so I would minimize the number of times per month that I had to travel to south Florida from Massachusetts. This was critical because the number of allowed free employee passes was limited during that first probationary year.

My first trip had a flight-engineer instructor who watched to make sure I was doing my job correctly. We got along just fine. The captain was an interesting guy, a bit of a cowboy, which was common in the old days. He would run the cockpit as he saw fit and aggressively chase after some of the new young flight attendants. On my very first layover, I remember the senior flight attendant pulling me aside and very sternly saying, "Let me give you a piece of advice. Do not wear any part of your uniform during the layover." Apparently, some pilots were cheap and didn't usually bring a complete set of civilian attire. Message received, ma'am!

I guess I was going to have to bring more clothes and shoes. That was significant because our first suitcase was a big Samsonite with no wheels. You were really weighed down with a big suitcase in one hand and a heavy flight kit in the other. Later, when suitcases were being sold with wheels, we used to call them "Wimp Wheels."

One of the funny jokes we told each other during this probation year was "don't go home with food on your breath" because first-year pay was quite low. For me it was literally half what I was making in the air force.

I spent as little time as needed in southern Florida, and a few months later was able to bid a slot at the Boston base. Now I would only be an hour or so from work. But don't let that fool you. The Massachusetts Turnpike was a real bugger during rush hour and in inclement weather. Boston traffic was always heavy, and the "Big Dig" was going on during my year in Boston. It made for some stressful commutes.

I also found that living in the Berkshire Mountains in Westfield, Massachusetts, was no easy life in the winter. I was driving a 1977 Chevrolet Monte Carlo, a V8 with rear-wheel drive, that I bought after graduating college in Miami. I would get about halfway up the mountain during the snowy winter months and usually end up in a snowbank. Then I would leave the car there and trudge the rest of the way to the house. At least I had my wife and kids in a four-wheel-drive Chevy Suburban. No glutton for punishment, as soon as my probation year ended, I bought myself a new four-wheel-drive Jeep.

The trips were fun though. We flew all over the US. Tampa, Detroit, Dallas, Los Angeles, Salt Lake City, and Seattle were constant destinations. Many of the flight attendants were former Northeast Airlines, and they were an older, crusty bunch, some of whose language could make a sailor blush.

I remember the first time I flew to Salt Lake City, a former Western Airlines base, and went down to the joint pilot/flight attendant lounge. This huge open space for both sets of flight crew was eye-opening. Delta was a conservative, old-fashioned company. I immediately thought to myself, *this will never do*. I was right. Shortly thereafter Delta put up a wall and separated the two groups.

Many of the Boston captains were also former Northeast Airlines, and quite a few of them were cowboys too. One was so irritating with his nit-picking demands that no one wanted to fly with him. It got so bad that scheduling would only accept a monthly bid directly from him over the phone, since others tried to bid his schedule so they could avoid him.

I flew a trip with one captain who had a voice exactly like Rodney Dangerfield. He was married to a flight attendant but did not seem to like any of those we flew with. He would verbally chew on them, and I would follow behind and tell them, "Hey, we're not all like that. Please don't forget to feed us!"

We had one layover in Baltimore with a super early pickup the next day, so early that the security gates on the concourses would still be locked when we got to the airport. One flight attendant was a couple of minutes late for the pickup. This captain called her room from the front desk and told her she was late. Instead of just saying she was on the way, she said, "Well, by my watch I show I still have three minutes to go." The captain about screwed himself into the ceiling. When she got down to the van, the only seat available was right next to him. As soon as she sat down, he turned to her and demanded an apology. Not a good way to start the day.

The next day we laid over in Little Rock. Only one elevator went to the floor where there was a crew room with breakfast laid out. I waited forever for that elevator to arrive and deliver me to the lobby.

By the time I got to the van, everyone else was already seated. I threw my bags in the back and took a seat in the back of the van. As the captain started to turn around and give me a load of grief, I cut him off by saying, "No worries, boss. By my watch I show I have three minutes to go." He just looked at me for a few seconds, smiled, then turned back around. Ballsy, but it worked.

On another trip we were approaching the gate in LAX. Western had started a new terminal and Delta finished it. It was called the "Oasis" and was very nice. I thought the aircraft's left wing was going to come very close to overrunning a fuel truck and started to say something. The captain immediately cut me off with, "Be quiet. It's hard to fly this thing from back there." Ouch!

It was a different world in the 1980s, and it would take some terrible accidents before all the airlines changed their culture and embraced the concepts of CRM (crew resource management) to better utilize the skills and expertise of all the resources available to crew members in the cockpit.

I was itching to get an assignment to a copilot's seat and finally bid the DC-9 in Cincinnati, Ohio. I was in my twelfth month with Delta and down in Atlanta for my annual B-727 training. I literally got pulled out of class by my chief pilot, who told me my training could be waived to the thirteenth month, which was when I would start DC-9 school, and he needed me for a trip in Boston the next day. So, back to Boston I went for one of my last trips as a flight engineer on the B-727.

I went down to Atlanta in August of 1988 for the DC-9 school. Delta put me in a hotel near the training center and the classroom was intimate: just four of us new copilots and the instructor, a former lead mechanic. We learned the systems in depth in the old days, taught to us by our own senior mechanics. That went right along with my military way of thinking.

We also had some fun while in training. You must remember that most of us came from a military background. Because our missions had a high level of risk, military pilots tended to be brutally honest with each other's mistakes, and the banter could be equally harsh. You just learned to develop thick skin, listen to the things that matter, and let the rest roll off your back.

One day in class our instructor, a nice young newlywed named Bob, was telling us a story about how he lived in a new neighborhood and a neighbor recently had a house fire. When the guy called 911 to report it, the local fire department had trouble finding the house. We said we could have found the house, but Bob said, "Not likely." Well, Bob had just thrown down the gauntlet. I went out on a reconnaissance mission that very afternoon and found the house without a problem.

We have an old tradition in the USAF called a "hospitality check." If we were in the officer's club on a Friday night and one of our squadron mates did not show up, we would go to his house and stomp on his roof until (A) the police showed up or (B) he let you inside. We would then drink all his liquor. After that you could guarantee a guy would show up when and where he was expected to be.

My DC-9 classmates and I drove to Bob's house on a Thursday night expecting him and his young bride to be home. They were not. Seems Bob had taken his wife to a movie. Being a resourceful former New Yorker, I promptly managed to get into his garage where they had left their lovable golden retriever. At least he seemed happy to see us. My class consisted of one Black and three White guys, all former military. I wrote a note and attached it to the dog's collar. It read *Dear Bob; we were here. Where were you? Love, Frankie and the White Boys.* We thought it had a nice ring to it!

Bob's wife was not nearly as amused when she let the dog in the house upon getting home. Bob came to class the next morning with a long face. We told him to be home that night, and we would come back to visit, and that is what we did. His wife took the whole joke quite well, we drank their beer, and then we left as friends. Looking back now, it isn't something I would do again, but it was our way of extending our tough friendship to Bob and his wife.

My first base in the DC-9 was Cincinnati. I found a captain with a big house in Covington, Kentucky, who had rooms for rent. He was divorced and spent a lot of time flying international and visiting his girlfriend in Germany. He wanted some people in the house on a regular basis since his ex-wife had once snuck in while he was away on a trip and emptied the place of furniture.

It was a truly beautiful, custom house on five wooded acres. There was a redwood solarium, a hot tub, and even a handball court! Three or four of us rented rooms. A beautiful German shepherd lived there in a large, fenced run in the backyard. I would bring it treats and steak bones and eventually we became constant companions. The owner even offered the dog to me when I finally left the Cincinnati base, but with three very young children at home, I did not feel I could trust the animal, so I regretfully declined.

I was very junior in my category, so I sat reserve for a year. It is very hard to appreciate sitting twenty days a month away from home, waiting for the phone to ring, and very rarely being called out to fly. Once again, I did not like being away from home so much and started thinking about bidding to the Atlanta base. Atlanta is the headquarters for Delta Air Lines, and it is also its largest hub. I would have better seniority and more varied opportunities to fly bigger equipment in the future. So, I got the bid and started planning the move from Massachusetts to Georgia.

It was not easy to sell the house in Massachusetts, but Rosann and I had already looked and found a new house in a small neighborhood in Kennesaw, Georgia, that we wanted. We signed a contract with a ninety-day contingency based on us selling the New England house. The good Lord shined on us, and we sold the house in December 1988.

I rented a big moving truck that we loaded ourselves with help from a neighbor's teenage boys. I did my last trip in Cincinnati, then the whole family piled into the moving truck and our car and drove a thousand miles to Atlanta in two days, arriving on the afternoon of New Year's Eve. We closed the same afternoon and unloaded the moving truck on New Year's Day, 1989.

I enjoyed the higher seniority in Atlanta. I was now flying a regular schedule each month. I look back at that operation and remember how we would pull into one gate, unload a hundred passengers, grab our bags, and hustle to another airplane on another concourse. Then we would preflight, load a hundred new passengers, and push back from the gate. All in forty minutes or less. We even flew up to seven legs a day. It was a busy but pleasurable time as a young copilot.

Delta was buying brand-new MD-88 aircraft from McDonnell Douglas at that time, so I bid into the category. This was going to be fun: new airplanes, glass displays, flight-management navigation systems. The training would be at the Long Beach production facility, and we would live in corporate apartments in nearby Seal Beach. So, off to California I went.

The month in Long Beach was very enjoyable. We got a tour of the McDonnell Douglas facility where MD-80 aircraft were assembled as well as the air force's C-17, which was just starting its production run. The simulator training was quite good, but I found it interesting that the instructors did not know the new flight-management navigation system (FMS) any better than we did. It was basically ignored. When I asked about the system, I was told, "You'll learn about that on the line."

At the very end of training, we had a check ride in the simulator that included a wind-shear scenario from a previous airline accident. I was the pilot flying, approaching the runway for landing, when the bottom dropped out of the airplane. I ended up not a hundred feet off the ground with the aircraft's nose pointed high in the air and only eighty knots of airspeed as I "walked" the aircraft out of danger. It looked much like the famous 1956 "Sabre Dance," an F-100 at Edwards AFB that crashed during landing, except I did not crash! I honestly believe the instructor was irritated that I "saved" the aircraft!

While at Long Beach I went to see the famous WWII *Queen Mary* cruise liner that was docked there, as well as the "Spruce Goose," Howard Hughes's giant H-4 Hercules amphibian that flew only once in November 1947. I have always been a fan of twentieth century history and particularly of our "Greatest Generation."

I met some very interesting fellow pilots during our stay at the Seal Beach apartments. His name escapes me, but one fellow copilot was a former British fighter pilot who did an exchange tour with the USAF and decided to stay. We played lots of tennis along with his captain, a Puerto Rican pilot who came up through the civilian ranks.

Sergio Rodrigo was a surprising guy. Of average height and a bit of a roly-poly, he played a wicked game of tennis by keeping me running all over the court! We became friends and I flew with him quite a bit over the next two years. I remember one trip where he wanted to debate the merits of allowing the burning of the American flag. Having served in the military for all my adult life, I had quite a different opinion than he did, and it caused some tension in the cockpit. Life is certainly about give and take, but my heart found it difficult to bear the thought of abusing the very symbol of our freedom.

Sergio was instrumental some years later while negotiating with a Puerto Rican–based cargo company for Delta Air Lines' original DC-3 aircraft. I heard it cost a million dollars plus a replacement DC-3. The aircraft was brought back to Atlanta and lovingly restored by Delta volunteers. It now sits in the museum at the Atlanta airport today.

A few years after the negotiation, I heard Sergio was killed. He ran a side business in aviation and died in a helicopter crash in South America. Many of our pilots are remarkable people with plenty of intelligence, drive, and other interests. Sergio's death was a reminder that commercial aviation is still considered one of the highest-risk occupations in the world. I was sorry to hear of his demise and think about him to this day.

I enjoyed flying the line on the MD-88. Over the years many pilots bad-mouthed the aircraft, but I thought it was a good place to learn Delta's expanded domestic system and how to manage and operate a modern glass cockpit. The flight-management navigation system took a while to master since it was a bit of trial and error, learning it on the line. I liked the glass panel displays for their crisp symbology and efficient gathering of needed flight information. This was the wave of the future.

Flying out of Atlanta could be tough, with forty-minute turns which required hustling to a different aircraft on a different concourse. With typically four or five flights a day, you definitely earned your keep.

I enjoyed getting to know cities like Cincinnati, Indianapolis, Albuquerque, and even Toronto. Sure, places like New York, Chicago, and Los Angeles are exotic by comparison, but I liked seeing smaller cities. They were like hidden jewels, ignored by many, but I enjoyed searching out their treasures. University gymnasiums, museums, and local watering holes were lots of fun to find and enjoy.

CHAPTER 15

Southern Living

My wife Rosann and I struggled a bit during those first five years at Delta. The union and the company had negotiated a lower pay for us called the "B scale." This substandard wage scale was a scourge of the greater airline industry at the time and would finally be canceled just two months after I completed five years. In the meantime, Rosann stayed at home to raise our three children while I hustled at Delta and in the Air National Guard.

Somehow, I managed to set enough of a regular schedule one year to coach my son Rick's Little League baseball team. It was important to me that I do the things normal fathers do. I very much wanted to be a part of their lives, unlike my own father, who was not a part of mine. More on that later.

I also did some things just for me. I wanted to continue my martial arts training that I started when I was on active duty in Texas. Rosann and I enjoyed going out to dinner once a week and there was a Chinese restaurant in Marietta, Georgia, that was a favorite of ours. The maître d' was a fellow named Jason who ran his own Wing Chun academy.

I was particularly fascinated by this martial art form. According to legend, it was developed by a Chinese woman hundreds of years ago. Yim Wing Chun spurned a local warlord's marriage offer, saying she would only marry him if he could beat her in a fight. She was trained by a Buddhist nun whose inspiration for this new, close-range combat style had come from observing the confrontation between a snake and a crane.

I did not stay at this training for very long, and I did not achieve a high rank, but I loved the intense physical exercise and the possible benefit of being able to protect myself in the closed confines of a cockpit. I look back now and wonder what would have happened if all the pilots in the hijacked cockpits on 9/11 had been trained in Wing Chun.

When we moved into our new house in Kennesaw, Georgia, we ended up with next-door neighbors who both worked in the medical field. Trish was a nurse practitioner, and Barry was training to be a physician's assistant in anesthesiology. Trish said that I was riding a skateboard down our street with my son the first time she saw me. She said, "This guy looks like fun!"

My youngest daughter Diana became fast friends with their daughter Katie, and we four adults became inseparable. We played tennis together. We went out to eat often with Trish's large family. It was like being a part of their family, and I didn't realize until much later how much that meant to me.

People come and go in your life. Some stay for a very long time, some only stay for a short while. Each relationship serves a purpose, although you may not know what that purpose is until much later. Things started to sour between our families after a few years and the more Barry and Trish pulled away, the more I tried to draw them back in. It got so bad that I felt emotional pain every time I pulled in the driveway and looked over at their house. Finally, we just ignored each other for the last few years until we sold our house and moved.

Time has given me perspective, and perhaps some wisdom. I can see now that I needed my neighbors much more than they needed me. I wanted to be close friends, for them to be the surrogate family I was missing in my own life. It was unfair of me to expect such a thing.

I have learned to be friendly and helpful to my neighbors, but to not expect too much, and to give them their space. We moved to a beautiful new house in Cartersville, Georgia, after Diana graduated from high school and left for college. Our little cul-de-sac got together regularly in the beginning for barbecues and other dinners, but I had learned my lesson to not push our friendship on our neighbors. I imagine it's like dating at work. It's great until it isn't anymore. Our twenty plus years in the new house have been much better than the previous by applying just this little bit of wisdom.

CHAPTER 16

Mommy Dearest

My mother Lillian was married four times during her life. The first time was to my father, John Aliano. The second time was to Richard Hess. The third time was during my first year of college to Frank Loy. Frank was a divorcé who worked at the same company as my mother. The fourth and final marriage was to Lee Casimer, a widower from Chicago who lived in Flagler Beach, Florida. I helped move my mom to Florida after Frank died, but more on that later.

My mother was big on loyalty and expected us children to accept whatever she presented to us, even a new father. But relationships are harder to build than that, and I probably rebelled against my mother more than my brothers Tim and Ray did.

Mom told me about my father, John Aliano, when I was fifteen while she was in the middle of divorcing Richard Hess. I think she wanted to be sure I would stay loyal to her. My interest piqued; I asked if I could meet John. She arranged for us to travel to Connecticut for a weekend and for me to spend a day with him.

He showed me around the Bristol area, where he had basically spent his entire life, and I even got to meet his wife Viola and see his two very young children, Jeff and Ann. We exchanged a few letters after that weekend, but my mom wanted me to be satisfied with that one visit. Every time I asked her about getting together with John again, she did all she could to turn me off the idea. In the meantime,

I completed high school and received a scholarship to attend the Merchant Marine Academy at Fort Schuyler in the Bronx. I was just seventeen years old.

During the spring of my freshman year, Mom married Frank Loy. Frank had younger children than my brothers and I, and in hindsight I think he wasn't sure what to do with us. He and I argued frequently, and I could see that he had a temper that he struggled to control. I tried to just keep things civil for Mom's sake, since he seemed good for her.

We argued once when I was home from college, and he slammed the heavy wooden front door on my hand as I was leaving the house. I also found out later that my brother Tim ran interference for Ray when they got in trouble, taking the physical blows that were meant for the younger Raymond.

Frank's weakness, and what ultimately led to his untimely death, was a terrible case of diabetes that never seemed to be under control. He was constantly bouncing back and forth from needing sugar or insulin. He and my mom were both fifty-four when they decided to retire early and planned to move to Florida. Frank never made it. He ended up in the hospital with fluid in his heart and lungs. He came home but within days was right back in the hospital, where he died of the complications.

I was in the Atlanta Delta pilot lounge at 0500 on the morning he died. One of the schedulers, Baker Stearns, paged my name and told me to call home. I flew to New York and was at my mother's house that same afternoon.

On the drive from the New York airport to Mom's house, I stopped by her brother's house in North Babylon. Uncle Duane and Aunt Maddie were favorites of mine when I was a kid. I lived in my grandparents' house when he was still in high school, and I always thought Maddie was so beautiful with her pretty face and red hair. Nana and Papé were wonderful, warm people, and as the matriarch, Nana seemed to hold the family together. It wasn't until she died that the infighting began.

My grandparents didn't have much money as they approached retirement, so they arranged to build an apartment in their garage and give the house to Duane and Maddie. The arrangement worked out fine until Nana died and Papé decided to move to Arizona to be near his other two daughters, Deane and Barbara. Papé needed to sell his furniture, but Duane and Maddie wanted several items. I was told my mother and my kid brother, Raymond, entered their house one evening to find Maddie with her hands around my grandfather's neck, verbally browbeating him. Lillian never forgave her brother or his wife.

I stopped at my uncle's house and told him about Frank's death. Naive me, I honestly thought that if ever there was a time to bury the hatchet and forgive, that time was now. My uncle asked me, "So, what does your mother think about that?" It was obvious to me that my uncle was not going to risk reaching out to his sister, only to be rejected. Oh well, I tried, but the lesson I learned repeatedly is that most people fear emotional confrontation and go out of their way to avoid conflict.

It was an interesting week at my mother's house. I watched her emotions swing from sadness to depression to anger. She barked at me only once. It was enough for me to tread lightly for the rest of that week.

Something that really surprised me was the reaction of my two brothers. Tim had gone into the basement and separated out a huge pile of Frank's tools and equipment that he wanted. Raymond had gone into Frank's clothes closet and taken all the clothes he wanted. The guy wasn't even in the ground yet and all his worldly possessions were being fought over by a couple of vultures. Unfortunately, I would see more of this behavior in later years.

The Bible says you can't serve two masters. My two brothers were showing me they cared more about physical things than they did about the people left behind in the wake of Frank's death. I would also see this kind of greed on a larger scale years later when I owned an aircraft maintenance business. It always amazed me how intensely some extremely wealthy people cared about preserving nickels and dimes while your small business limped away bloody from the deal.

When Frank Loy died it seemed to change my whole relationship with my mother. I believe Lillian needed a man in her life and I became her surrogate. We started getting along very well. I called her often and she also called often to ask my advice on any number of matters. After four decades I was enjoying being close to Mom again. I hadn't felt this close to her since I was fifteen and she had divorced Richard Hess.

Mom had bought a liquor store near the train station in Lindenhurst and continued running it by herself. I remember coming home on holidays and helping her stock the shelves. She would always say, "Remember, Richie, make them bend over for the cheap stuff!" The good stuff was always chest-high. Funny lady.

After a few years Mom decided she wanted to sell her house in West Islip and complete her original plan to move to Florida. She found a new neighborhood being built in Palm Coast, just south of St. Augustine. She sold the New York house and business, and I helped her move into her new house. She seemed happy and quickly established herself with friends and activities. It didn't hurt that her cousin Beverly lived only a few minutes away. Mom and Beverly had grown up together and were inseparable as teenagers.

My positive relationship with her continued during this time. She dated a little but nothing serious. I traveled to Florida often to see her, as did Rosann and our kids. She continued to rely on me for advice as she dealt with the many things that come with moving and owning a home. I was truly enjoying my role, and then everything changed.

Mom started dating Lee Casimer, and it quickly became evident they were getting serious. Their relationship was new, but we are talking about people in their sixties and seventies, since he was a decade older than Mom. Also, Lee had other "lady friends" and Mom placed a high priority on loyalty, so this became a major issue. She called me one day to discuss her concerns and I remember saying teasingly to her, "You sound like the relationship is serious. So, when are you going to marry this guy?" She vehemently disagreed with my assessment, and I let it go.

A month later Mom called to announce that she and Lee would be getting their respective affairs in order over the next six months, and then they were planning to get married. I suspected this was going to happen all along, so her call did not surprise me. I had met Lee, and I thought he was a very nice man. However, a couple of weeks later she called again to say they were getting married in a few weeks.

Suddenly alarm bells were going off in my head, and I was thinking, *Is there something wrong here? Is Lee trying to somehow take advantage of Mom? Do I need to do something to protect her?*

So, I asked her, "What's the rush? I thought you were going to wait six months?" Well, you would have thought I had slapped her in the face. She told me in no uncertain terms that this was none of my business! I had been the man in her life since Frank died, and suddenly I was no longer needed in that role. So, I backed off and went along with her plans quietly.

Shortly after they got married, Mom called me one Sunday night. She sounded drunk and made vague complaints about Lee. I was concerned enough that I immediately made plans to fly down to Florida the next day and find out what was going on.

We sat at Mom's sunroom table for lunch, and I asked them to explain what was going on. It turned out they were having all the same problems any new relationship has—but these were now elderly people, who had already built entire lives, dealing with something more common to young people, who are just paving their way. Both wanted to preserve their wealth for their children's inheritance. Both needed to contribute to the monthly living expenses. Both needed to get used to being around another adult with their own ideas about how things should be handled.

I tried to be fair and listen to both sides, but as Mom explained to me in a phone call a few days later, she was disappointed I didn't automatically take her side. There was that loyalty issue again.

As I have mentioned before, when Lillian got angry, she would often grab her car keys and go for a long ride until she cooled off. She had done this since I was a kid. Lee didn't understand that about her, and he worried she would get into an accident while in that state of mind. So, when the argument got heated, she grabbed her car keys while Lee tried to physically restrain her.

While discussing this in my presence, Mom got so angry again that she threw a glass of water in Lee's face. It shocked me, and I had to jump between them to keep her from scratching his eyes out. Neither Lee nor I realized just how vicious she could be when aroused. Some years later I remarked that when she got angry with someone, she immediately tried to extract a pound of flesh. She responded, "Damn right!"

I arranged for them to see a doctor if only to be sure both were in good health. I also laid out some ideas about how they could both draw up new wills and establish a new joint checking account, which they could contribute to for day-to-day living expenses. When I finally left, they were holding hands and seemed to have gotten past their newlywed crisis. Thank goodness.

During these early years of Mom and Lee's marriage, they traveled to Atlanta a couple of times to visit me and my family. Mom smoked her entire adult life and had started complaining about circulation issues before she moved out of New York. Rosann's father also smoked his whole adult life and had one leg amputated due to loss of circulation. I was worried for my mother and tried to convince her to quit, but to no avail. Every time I visited her in Florida, or when she came to Atlanta, she would wander off to a bedroom or bathroom and suddenly the whole house would reek of tobacco.

On her last visit to our house during one very hot summer, I woke in the middle of the night to the smell of her smoking and found a window in the guest room open even though it was ninety degrees outside. I said something to her later that day and of course she denied she was smoking in the house. Rosann and I had to run an errand, and when we got home that afternoon, Lee and Mom were gone. I was obviously a slow learner and did not realize that, as far as she was concerned, I was being disrespectful and disloyal every time I opened my mouth to challenge her. Things were about to get much worse.

As I was approaching my fortieth birthday, I was thinking more and more about my father John. Every time I mentioned it to Lillian, she would talk me out of it. I was trying to be respectful of her wishes, but I just felt there was an empty hole inside of me that only John could fill. I finally found his phone number from Connecticut information, but first I told Mom I was going to make the call. As a loyal son, I felt I had an obligation to tell her before I called him.

Lillian tried one last time to stop me, but I felt it was something I had to do. As I look back, I am very glad I made that call. It was a good relationship for a few short years, but it's hard to go back four decades and pick up where you left off. John's wife Viola felt her children's place was threatened by my presence, and I later learned she told her children ugly things about me that were not true.

In the meantime, I learned some new things about myself. John and I had many of the same likes and dislikes. In fact, the first time I flew up to Hartford to meet him, we walked out to the parking lot to his pickup truck. It was my pickup truck: make, model, color. Spooky!

The ways John and I reacted to certain circumstances were also identical. We had the same color eyes. Viola once told Rosann, "It's weird looking into another man's face and seeing my husband's eyes." Even my grandfather, whom I never met and was long dead, had certain habits that I found out were identical to my own. Most people think we are shaped strictly by our environment, but I know differently. We are programmed to a great degree at the moment of conception. It took getting to know my father to understand that fact.

I suffered the loss of my mother because of my perceived disloyalty.

She started ignoring me and my children, and she developed a closer relationship with my brothers and theirs. I don't blame them. It was my own fault for not being able to be the son Lillian wanted. I wanted to know my father and had a typical type A personality: aggressive and questioning. That doesn't make me a bad person. It just means that I was never going to live up to Lillian's expectations.

I tried for the next decade to crack the shell Mom put up but was never able to do so. I called her once and somehow got on the subject of her will. As her oldest child, I had been her executor for years. She told me she had changed her will and appointed Raymond as her new executor. In fact, she had done so shortly after I looked up my father. My brothers knew but didn't dare tell me, it seems, for fear of suffering the same fate. I hung up the phone, went into my bedroom, and cried my eyes out.

I told Rosann that all of this would not be over until Lillian died. I don't know how I knew that, but I felt sure it was true. I was not going to change her mind or make her care about me and my family no matter how much I wanted her to. I could not have known how right I was until she passed away.

I got a call from Raymond one day saying that Mom had been admitted to the hospital. She started having speech problems and the doctors found a sizable tumor in her brain. They removed it successfully, but I knew that typically a brain tumor starts elsewhere in the body and metastasizes. After her operation they did a battery of tests and concluded Lillian was riddled with cancer. They gave her a prognosis of six months. She did not last six weeks.

Raymond called me again when Mom was days away from passing away. Rosann and I dropped everything and drove to Florida immediately. Lillian was in bad shape. She could not take care of herself. She was wearing diapers and was reduced to sitting in a chair or lying in bed. Rosann and I did what we could to care for her and she died a few days later.

The day after she was buried, Raymond read her will. In it she specifically stated, "I have left nothing for my son, Richard Hess, for reasons best known to us all." For my disloyalty of allowing John back in my life, I was not just purged from her life but also disinherited from her estate. It's not as if I needed her money. It just felt like such an unfair and vindictive thing to do. I faced my two brothers and told them I felt it was a terrible thing for them to have gone along willingly with her plan for revenge. Neither of them had anything to say, and they haven't communicated with me since that day even though I've reached out to them. You cannot serve two masters.

While there are moments when I look back on all of this and wish for a different story, I realize I cannot change other people. Sure, I miss my brothers. They were good company growing up and in the early adult years. But money changes people. Even Lee said later that Mom's view of me grew harsher after a visit from my kid brother and his wife. I was shocked, wondering what they could have said that might have turned my own mother against me.

The result is that I am scrupulously fair with my own three children. If I give something to one, I do the exact same thing for the other two. My gifts or generosity may be different depending on the circumstances, but I'll be damned if I will ever do to my children what was done to me. They are all different, and I cannot say I like or agree with everything they say or do, but they are my family, and I want them to learn a better way to behave.

When I am dead and gone, I hope they will remember these lessons about fairness and vindictiveness I tried to teach them, because the alternative in my life was a pain so deep and personally violating that I would not wish it even on a hated enemy.

CHAPTER 17

A Yankee Comes to Town

When I moved the family to Atlanta in 1988, I started looking for an Air National Guard or Air Force Reserve unit closer to my new home. It had been difficult to travel all the way to New England and keep up with all the currency requirements, especially during the winter months. To average six sorties, I was spending twelve days at the unit each month. I needed to find something closer.

I talked to several fighter units at first, including the A-10 reserves in Belle Chasse, Louisiana, and the RF-4 unit in Birmingham. I nearly had a slot wrapped up in Birmingham until the operations officer said I would have to move to the local area. I had just bought a house in Kennesaw, Georgia, and they wouldn't allow me to commute the two-hour drive. Oh well.

I also talked to a few transport units including the C-130 guard unit in Savannah and the C-130 reserve unit in Montgomery. The Alabama unit offered me a slot, but I put them off, hoping for a fighter slot. By the time I got back to them, the offer had been withdrawn. I couldn't blame them.

I finally contacted the C-141 guard unit in Jackson, Mississippi. I had flown the type on active duty in New Jersey five years previously, and I'd heard good things about the unit. I sent a nice application package and received a positive response almost immediately. I was invited to come out for a visit during their next drill weekend.

The people in the squadron seemed very nice. Some of the senior people sort of looked at me as if I was an intruder, but most of the leadership seemed to recognize that I had a lot of experience to offer. By Sunday afternoon I had been offered, and accepted, an opportunity to join the unit and train locally in the aircraft.

I read the flight manual, and it didn't take me long to process into the unit and become requalified in the aircraft. In fact, it was easy getting back into an aircraft I already had a couple of thousand hours in and had previously been qualified as an aircraft commander.

My first trip out of the local area was a weeklong mission in support of the Hawaii Army National Guard. We flew to just about every Hawaiian island and stayed at Hickam AFB on Oahu. I had never been to Hawaii before this trip, so I really enjoyed the experience. We visited bars and restaurants in Waikiki every night. A side note: The operations building dated back to before WWII and still had bullet holes from the Pearl Harbor attack!

Our favorite spot was the Shorebird at the west end of Waikiki. They had a karaoke bar and cheap mai tais. I had a few drinks, sang a karaoke song, and even thought I was pretty good. I went back the next night totally sober and did it again. Not so good. I learned my lesson and retired from karaoke.

Being in a time zone six hours earlier than back home, I found I could not sleep much past three or four in the morning. So, I would call the copilot's room, wake him up, and make him go out jogging along Waikiki Beach. To this day I appreciate his good humor and accommodating nature. The best part was seeing all the older Asian people who would come down to the beach to practice tai chi. Their movements were very beautiful to watch. We would jog or hike as far as Diamond Head, a ten-mile round trip!

Our aircraft commander was a crusty old lieutenant colonel. I was a first pilot at that time, qualified in both seats. On the morning we were to fly home, the commander showed up quite hungover. I put him in a spare seat in the cockpit and told him I would let him know if I needed him.

I climbed into the left pilot seat and called for the "before starting engines checklist." The copilot looked at me and began to say, "What about the colonel . . ."

I told him, "Shut up. Just run the checklist." The colonel got into one of the bunks and slept a few hours while we got our clearance, climbed up to altitude, and entered our oceanic track back to the mainland. A few hours later the colonel came back on the flight deck and thanked me for covering for him.

Covering for each other was something we did in the service without having to be told. As the years have gone by, most of us have matured, plus our society has become less tolerant of immature behavior. But sometimes the circumstances are beyond your control.

I get ahead of myself, but at least twice, both times in India, I have come to the aid of a sick or injured crew member. The first time was when a flight attendant inadvertently walked into a floor-to-ceiling glass wall. The glass was so clean that she did not see it until it was too late. I thought she had broken her nose, so we arranged with the hotel to have her seen by a doctor.

The second time was when I was a captain on the B-777. We were on a forty-eight-hour layover in Mumbai (Bombay). With any flight of more than twelve hours, we would have two captains and two first officers. The other captain went out of the hotel to have a sandwich the evening before our nighttime departure. He got very bad food poisoning. I was the pilot flying us home, so I spent the first four hours of an eighteen-hour flight in the cockpit while he went to the bunk to sleep.

When he came back into the cockpit to relieve me, I remember telling him, "You look like hell. There's no way I'm sleeping where you've been, and second, there's no way I'm leaving you in charge. Go back to bed. I'll see you in Atlanta." So that's what we did. He slept the whole way home, we swapped copilots every four hours, and I rested in my pilot seat when I needed a nap. We made it work.

I stayed in the Mississippi Air National Guard for twelve years before retiring in 2002. I progressed from captain to major to lieutenant colonel and retired as a guard colonel. My duties included being an aircraft commander, instructor pilot, evaluator pilot, air refueling IP, deployment commander, flight commander, squadron commander, and chief of the standardization and evaluation section.

As a unit we participated in many operational missions. These included Desert Storm, post-9/11 Middle East operations, and numerous other worldwide operations and relief efforts. I was brand new to the unit when Desert Shield kicked off in 1990. I remember my first trip into the desert, looking out at that vast moonscape, and thinking, *this is not worth American lives.*

I was paired with Mike Brock, a fellow Delta pilot. Mike hated cold weather. While the rest of us were dying of the heat in the Arabian Desert, Mike was happy as a clam at 120 degrees Fahrenheit. We would pile blankets and jackets in his lap during flights to keep him from turning the flight deck into a sauna! I would tell him he's an alien with insides rearranged like Spock from *Star Trek*. He would respond, "Cool comes from the inside out!"

After a few months I was given my own crew, and we completed ten months of support for the forces operating in the desert. We went everywhere and hauled everything. Turkey, Jordan, Israel, Bahrain, Oman, UAE, Saudi Arabia, and Qatar were constant destinations. We carried food, water, ammunition, bulldozers, and troops. We lived in communal tents and worked thirty-hour workdays.

I remember being on alert one day at Torrejón Air Base in Madrid, Spain, when my crew was called for a mission that had been turned down by another crew. We were to fly to the Middle East to a set of coordinates and call on a certain frequency. We would then be given landing information. We flew to a point in the UAE, I made the call, and a British voice gave us a navigation frequency to monitor. Turns out we were only the second aircraft to land at a brand-new airport the US had built for this very purpose.

By the end of ten months, I was very tired. It wasn't just the grueling schedule of 150 flight hours every month. We had been exposed to oil fires, strong insect repellents, and supposedly some chemical weapons. I returned home in May 1991 exhausted, with unexplained skin rashes and a spine that felt like it had been hit by a hammer along its length. The symptoms were called Gulf War syndrome, and it took a year before they magically evaporated all on their own.

Between the end of Desert Storm in May 1991 and the 9/11 attack in 2001, I worked at Delta and began to take on more and more responsibilities at the guard unit. I generally liked the people and the missions. As I rose in rank and quickly approached a retirement point, the unit seemed interested in giving me positions with more say in how operations were conducted. That was always a big carrot to dangle in front of any hardworking, type A personality. You worked your entire career just to get to the point where you finally had some control.

The leadership positions in the unit were like having another full-time job. I was living in Atlanta, flying full-time for Delta, trying to be a husband and a father, and working to make a difference at the unit with my newly awarded responsibilities. I even applied to and was accepted to law school at Georgia State University. I should teasingly say I didn't know what I wanted to be when I grew up, but something had to give.

The first sacrifice was money. As you gained seniority at my airline, you had opportunities for overtime flying at double the normal hourly rate. I had to turn down more flying than I care to remember due to prior obligations at the guard unit.

The second sacrifice was family. It was not until after I retired that I realized just how much time the guard took away from my personal life. When you are away from home fifteen to sixteen days a month with your airline job and then add another seven to ten days a month on military duty, it adds up to only being home one or two days a week at best.

Rosann and I started to have problems. We argued a lot, and I buried myself in my work, resulting in more and more time away from home. There were even a few times I left home for a couple of weeks at a time, thinking I wasn't happy in my marriage. I contemplated a permanent separation from Rosann but never seemed able to commit to that decision. Thank God, because looking back, my life would have been far worse without the love of my wife and family.

No matter how hard I tried not to, I finally came to realize that I still loved Rosann very much. I also realized my problems were not external ones. That was just an excuse. I was searching outside of myself for a solution to problems that lay strictly inside of me.

As I described earlier, I had a very difficult relationship with my mother for many years. It seems that relationship warped me to the point that I didn't seem capable of a decent relationship with any woman. It wasn't until my mom died that I began to heal myself. Now, more than two decades after Mom died, Rosann and I have known each other fifty-three years and the relationship is better than it's ever been before. I thank God every day that we survived those troubled times.

I remember exactly where I was when the 9/11 attacks occurred. By then I was a B-737-800 captain and scheduled to fly to the West Coast that morning. I was literally on my way to the Atlanta airport when scheduling called and told me to go home, that my trip had been canceled. I got home and turned on the TV to watch the Twin Towers come down. It was a horrible, helpless feeling.

I knew what was coming, so I packed my suitcase and drove six hours to Mississippi. The very next morning the unit assembled two crews, and we were on our way to Germany, where we set up a staging operation. Buster Sweeny, the other aircraft commander, and I were like a wrestling tag team. One would operate the stage, getting the aircraft, cargo load, and flight planning ready for the other crew, who would fly to the Middle East and back. Then when they got back to Germany, we would have the aircraft serviced and loaded in two hours, and we would do a similar mission to the desert and back. We did that for a couple of weeks until Washington, DC, activated the whole unit.

I certainly flew my share of missions into the Middle East. I remember one night mission out of Germany in the middle of a snowstorm. We worked for over twenty-four hours straight. The wing flaps had moisture from the blizzard, resulting in being locked in the up position, requiring a 200-mph landing speed. Then the copilot's flight instruments failed on the flight back to Germany. Finally, when we configured for landing in Frankfurt, one of the aircraft's main landing gears did not extend properly. We finally got the gear down and landed safely.

On another mission, I was asleep in the bunk as we approached the Egyptian coast from Europe. Suddenly I was shaken awake by one of my flight engineers. I sat on the jump seat between the two other pilots and scanned the engine instruments. One of the four engines had blown a carbon seal and was about to shed itself over the Mediterranean. I quickly directed the engine to be shut down and the crew to descend to a lower altitude.

We turned away from North Africa and considered possible landing sites in Turkey, Greece, and Italy. One of the pilots suggested going back to Germany, but I decided to land in Sicily instead. The last thing we needed to do was fly a few more hours with an engine shutdown, over the Alps, to land in a snowstorm.

The airplanes were approaching forty years old and over forty thousand flight hours. They were getting very old and very tired. We would later find out we were having issues with wing cracks, windshield-frame cracks, fuel leaks, and numerous lesser issues. The C-17 production was going strong and not a day too soon! It was time to retire the Starlifters.

I ran the staging operation at Ramstein Air Base, Germany, for several months in 2002. Considering the operations tempo and the age of the airlift fleet, we managed to set several records. In fact, while I was running the staging operation, we managed to operate the best aircraft in-commission rate, the best on-time-departure rate, and the best mission-completion rate of any airlift operation in the Military Airlift Command for the previous twelve years. When I finally came home and told my wife about our accomplishment, she said, "You can retire now. You don't have anything left to prove."

Rosann was right, but it would take another event to convince me to finally retire. We had an African American pilot from New Jersey who had joined the unit. Ben Salley was relatively new but had thousands of hours as a civilian flight instructor. I was convinced he would be a great aircraft commander if just given the chance. I scheduled him for an upgrade school and planned to put him with a strong crew to season him during this post-9/11 activation.

The unit was scheduled to transition to the C-17, and I was asked to be part of the initial cadre. That was a real vote of confidence. One of our generals pulled me aside and told me I would make general if I continued what I was doing and just kept my nose clean. Things were really looking up.

I was running the staging operation in Germany when I learned that Ben's upgrade school had been canceled without my knowledge. It seemed there were some people who thought Ben wasn't spending enough time at the unit after he got hired by the airlines and was therefore unworthy of the upgrade. I was angry beyond belief at this situation and made my feelings known to the group and wing commanders.

I had a meeting with my bosses when I returned from Germany, and it did not go well. They felt I should be more supportive of their decisions, and I thought they should be more supportive of my judgment when it came to managing my people. In the end, my position as the squadron commander was not tenable. I was relieved of command, and I immediately decided to retire.

In retrospect, I can look back at that situation and see exactly what

I did wrong. More than twenty years brings a certain wisdom. I did not handle the situation well. That is not to say what happened to Ben was right, but I ignored the politics of working with my superiors. I allowed my personal irritation to interfere with good judgment.

From every bad situation comes something good. The way Ben's situation was handled became an issue that rose to the state level, and eventually that decision's perpetrator was made to leave the unit. Ben eventually moved to Houston with his airline. He is a well-respected union representative and serves to this day with a UAV (drone) unit nearby.

And I got my life back. As I said, I never realized how much my family sacrificed because of my guard duty until I retired. Suddenly, I had time on my hands like never before. I could go to work for Delta, fly my trip, then come home and do things with my family. Rosann and I took trips, visited our adult children and friends, and rediscovered each other. Retirement from the guard was the best thing I could have done. My only wonder, with hindsight being 20/20, was why I did not do it sooner.

I served a total of twenty-eight years in the US Air Force and Air National Guard. I flew trainers, transports, and fighters. I served in nine war zones and relief efforts. I earned a BS and master's degree, as well as all my advanced pilot licensing. Yes, they were years of sacrifice, but also years of accomplishment. If I had it all to do over again, I might make some different decisions. However, I am extremely proud of all I did, and I regret none of it. After all, we are partially defined by what we accomplish.

Photo Gallery

Praha, Czech Republic

Perth, Australia

L-39 in Australia

Praha, Czech Republic

Quito, Equador with Diana

All the Girls

Prague

Bodo, Norway

Ukraine 2012

The Girls

Rio de Janeiro

Kano, Nigeria maintenance team

Borneo with Rosann, Ann, and Diana

Bob Lutz's L-39 Albatros

Waycross, February, 2016

Churchill Dinner, 2016

Gulu, Uganda Maintenance Team

Feeding a Giraffe

Waycross 2018

Bob Lutz's Alpha Jet

Masai Warriors

Aviation University, China

Delta Last Flight, 2018

Ukranian AN-12 with Ariel Ludie

Josie and Charlie

Rich with Sister Ann

GA Mountains

Bundled Up

Grand View, Antarctica

Six Adventures

On the Bridge

Cirrus Ride, 2024

CHAPTER 18

If It Ain't Boeing, I Ain't Going

When the air force released my guard unit from active duty after the first Desert Storm in May 1991, I was approaching four years with Delta Air Lines. I had sat on the B-727 engineer's seat for one year, spent one year as a DC-9 copilot, and finished two years as an MD-88 copilot. Now it was time to move up to the big leagues.

A couple of months after I returned from the desert I got a slot on the combined B-757/B-767 fleet. I would stay on that fleet for six years. I already mentioned the B-scale pay rates we suffered through for the first five years. Couple that with the threat of being called up to active military duty and you found yourself being very careful with money, because if you lived on the financial edge, you might end up behind the proverbial financial eight ball if called up.

The training on the 757/767 fleets went very well. Our ground school was still being conducted by former Delta lead technicians. I really loved learning the airplanes in depth. What I did find a little daunting was that I would be qualified on more than one type of aircraft at once. By the time I left the fleet to become a captain six years later, there were something like six or eight different combinations of airframe, engine, navigation system, and systems enhancements. You might not fly a particular type of aircraft for months and then suddenly find yourself flying one. It was important to know the differences.

Also, the simulators were a bit more basic back in those days.

They mostly had nighttime visual displays. On later fleets we would experience the latest computer-generated day and night displays that were uncanny in their similarity to real-world visual cues.

Over the thirty-one years I flew for Delta, I had really come to love Boeing airplanes. I later became an instructor and evaluator in the B-757/B-767 category and was constantly impressed with the capabilities of these fleets. More on that later.

As a wide-body copilot I got to do even more extended flying and began to see more of the big cities in the US, Canada, and Mexico, as well as some of the island destinations in the Caribbean. I also flew with some very interesting captains.

One captain was a physics major in college, and we spent an entire month discussing his favorite person, "One Cup," (Einstein . . . get it?) and concepts of quantum leap, the theory of relativity, and other such esoteric topics. Another captain actively restored and flew pre-WWII German aerobatic aircraft.

One memorable captain rode his Harley-Davidson motorcycle from Atlanta to the end of the Alaska Highway in Fairbanks and back home again one summer! This same guy climbed mountains all over the world. He was planning to hike to the top of Mount Kilimanjaro in East Africa, and when I said I had spent some time in Kenya he said, "We don't have anyone on the team who has been to East Africa. Want to go?" I asked how long the trip would be and he remarked, "About a month."

When I came home and asked Rosann, she said, "Heck no!"

Funny, because I also had an opportunity to fly a DC-3 right seat one summer when they pulled Glacier Girl, a P-38 from the WWII "Lost Squadron," out of the Greenland ice cap. I came home and asked Rosann if I could spend two weeks on the ice, and again she said, "Heck no!" Gosh, she was no fun at all!

After a couple of years flying Boeings for Delta, I had an opportunity to join the training department. I taught in the classroom for a few years and flew the line on a part-time basis. We taught flight attendant leadership, as well as pilot and flight attendant security and crew resource management (CRM) courses. CRM was just getting started as the industry sought to standardize how crews worked together to handle things like communication, decision-making, and time management, all in a concerted effort to increase safety and decrease accident rates.

I enjoyed the classroom environment. I had run a ground school for student pilots while at the air force UPT program at Sheppard AFB, Texas, in the mid-eighties, so it was a bit like coming home. Plus, I had the added benefit of being home most nights. My children were young, one each in high school, middle school, and elementary school. I love flying, but being away from home half the month gave me a sense of separation from the family, and I wanted desperately to be closer to them.

The classrooms could be lively. We had just merged with the remnants of Pan American World Airways and we had flight attendants from Poland, India, and Israel. I was particularly impressed with the Israeli flight attendants. Israelis live or die by their security awareness. When we did security classes, they were always right on top of the situation. When we showed videos of security scenarios, they would catch every detail and be able to relay all pertinent information to the designated captain. If I ever had a security problem, I wanted those flight attendants on my crew!

One thing led to another, and Delta was trying to reduce costs in the simulator programs. They opened the instructor cadre to copilot candidates. I applied and was accepted to the 757/767 program.

I got off to a slow start being an instructor. You would have thought I'd be a natural at it since I'd done similar work during two tours in the air force, but it didn't work out that way. I wasn't getting along with the program head very well. I felt he was hard to please, and when he would monitor my sim sessions, his debriefs seemed overly critical.

The truth is I was too overbearing with my pilot crews, giving a lot of verbal corrections and not letting them learn from their own mistakes. After all, that's what the simulator was for, right? However, by the second year I really settled down and started to enjoy the newer, full-motion simulators with advanced visual displays.

As the instructor or PCA (proficiency check airman), I conducted all initial and recurrent training and got to play all the roles: controller, flight attendant, and other aircraft. It really was fun. Also, in the last year I was made an FAA designee check airman. The FAA does not have enough people to give every check ride in the civilian system, so experienced instructors and PCAs were designated to give many check rides. Each airline had a set of designees for each fleet.

Giving check rides was the only time I felt real stress on the job. Sometimes a guy just had a bad day, and I always felt stressed, holding his license in my hand and trying to get him to relax so he could meet the check ride requirements. I used to wear funny Looney Tunes or Tabasco ties, trying to bring the tension down a notch.

Thank goodness I didn't have to "bust" very many pilots. However, the head of the whole department once told us, "A check ride is like being an umpire in baseball. You have to call the balls and strikes." He also said, "If you wouldn't put your wife and kids on an aircraft that guy was flying that day, then he didn't pass." These were good words to remember when you weren't sure about a pilot's performance.

I was at the ten-year point in my career, and guys around me were starting to make captain. I had a couple of run-ins with some of the senior people in the department and wasn't as happy with my position as I had been. I later found out I had been too rigid while training some of my fellow instructors and they had a harsh opinion of me because I demanded such perfection. The reputation was well deserved, but at the time I didn't seem to realize what I was doing, nor was I able to control myself well enough to tone it down. It's okay to be demanding, but once again, I was impatient to correct them instead of allowing them to make such mistakes and handle the correction in the debrief.

Self-perception is a very difficult thing for most people, and I was no exception. Also, this career field of aviation has always been extremely intolerant of any sloppiness or inattention. My type A personality and obsessive behavior, while making me safer as a pilot, was getting in the way of my ability to teach students and get along with my peers. It was not until I left the training department that I became more aware of the problem and matured enough to control myself.

While I regret not having always served in the training department to the very best of my ability, I still appreciate that life and maturity should not become stagnant, no matter how old you are. People can and do learn from their mistakes. I humbly feel I am an example of that. However, becoming a better person, whether it is personal or professional, takes a lot of effort. It is not easy, it sometimes is not fun, and it takes courage. How many people do you know who can look in the mirror, see what is truly there, and commit to making themselves better? Many of the people I have met in my life seem more content with not looking in the mirror at all. The greatest courage a person can have is the willingness to see himself truthfully and want to change for the better.

CHAPTER 19

Mad Dog Captain

I was at about ten and a half years with Delta when I decided it was the right time to bid a captain's slot. Some airlines forced pilots to upgrade as others in their seniority moved up, but at Delta it was entirely up to the pilot to decide when to do so. After having been an instructor and evaluator in Delta's training department, I felt very ready, knowing exactly what the FAA and the company expected of a Delta captain.

As a copilot, we did plenty of actual training flights in the aircraft itself, such as the DC-9 and MD-88. However, simulators were getting more and more sophisticated every year, finally to the point that training flights were no longer necessary. We did all our training in the simulator and then went to "the line" for a few legs with a line-check airman. After that you were on your own.

By the time I made MD-88 captain, Delta had set up simulators in Atlanta for MD-88 and MD-90 aircraft. We would be dual qualified since the 90 had some significant differences in terms of systems as well as a different engine. I had one MD-90 simulator ride and then never flew the type again since it was only flown out of Dallas at the time. Thank goodness. I didn't really like the airplane and wanted to focus on what I had flown when I was an 88 copilot.

Something I enjoyed immensely was Delta's class for first-time captains called "In Command." Several instructors, senior captains, and management personnel (even the CEO) came in to talk to us about what was expected of a Delta captain. I remember one fellow telling us, "A Delta captain never has to get angry. He can stop an operation any time he thinks it is appropriate." I liked that idea. It is not a democracy, and like the captain of a ship, an airline captain is ultimately responsible for the operation.

The "Mad Dog" was a good place to cut my teeth as a new captain. The airplane was a development and upgrade of the old DC-9, with a longer fuselage, uprated engine, and a glass cockpit. However, this first-generation automation had its limitations, and it took a while to develop the technics to fly the airplane smoothly while on the autopilot. I also got to see many of the smaller cities that Delta served, such as Jackson, Mississippi; Shreveport and Monroe, Louisiana; Montgomery and Mobile, Alabama; and many others. We also got to spread our wings as far west as Albuquerque and Salt Lake City.

I experienced my fair share of mostly medical emergencies. Heart attacks, seizures, and even weather diversions happened with more regularity than you might think possible. I got very comfortable with calculating fuel requirements and even what to say to air traffic control (ATC) when I needed priority handling. I remember one heart attack incident while flying into Mobile. We declared an emergency and were flying much faster than normal as we approached the airport. ATC said, "Delta, you're ten miles from the airport and there is traffic on final. You're just gonna have to slow down!"

I responded, "No, sir. We have a medical emergency. Get that other aircraft out of our way!"

On another flight we were flying from Poughkeepsie, New York, to Atlanta. We were about eighty miles northeast of Knoxville, Tennessee, when one of my flight attendants called the cockpit to report that a passenger was having a grand mal seizure. There were a pair of nurses tending to the guy, so I turned to my copilot and said, "Your aircraft. Knoxville is eighty miles to your right. Tell, don't ask, ATC that you are diverting."

I coordinated all the other information with the cabin and the company and finally took over the airplane about ten miles from the airport. I was flying so fast that when I finally pulled the throttles to idle and deployed the speed brakes to slow down, I thought I had screwed up and would not get it slowed down in time to get the landing gear and flaps extended. Thank goodness it worked out.

We landed, taxied to the gate, deplaned the sick passenger and his wife, fueled, and redispatched to Atlanta in twenty minutes! Amazing what Delta flight control could do when they wanted the aircraft! Later that evening we flew the next leg to LaGuardia, New York. We ended up holding for a long time over the Carolinas due to thunderstorms in the New York area and finally diverted to Raleigh-Durham for fuel. What are the chances of two diversions in one workday? Go figure!

We also did quite a few sports charters on the Mad Dog. Professional baseball and college basketball teams were a nice break from the normal routine. I can tell you that we ate very well on those charter flights. Steaks, burgers, ice cream, and candy bars flowed like water! I also got a few baseballs autographed for my kids. It was good duty.

I flew the MD-88 for two years. Delta was expanding its fleet of B-737 aircraft at that time. I had an opportunity to bid on the B-737-300G (glass cockpit). It would be more money and a chance to get back into a Boeing aircraft, so I put my bid in and was scheduled for training. I felt reasonably seasoned now and was looking forward to learning about a new airplane.

CHAPTER 20

Flying the B-737

The B-737-300G was a small fleet that Delta bought from a European carrier. I don't think we ever had more than eighteen of these aircraft. What was interesting was that even though it was a -300, many of its parts were different from the original -300 aircraft Delta flew. So, Delta had to maintain a separate and unique parts inventory for a very small fleet, not a very efficient thing to do. Eventually that fact would lead to the -300Gs being retired early.

I enjoyed flying the type. The CFM56 engines were significantly quieter and more economical to operate than the JT8Ds used on the -100 and -200s. We flew to many of the same smaller and medium-size US cities that I saw on the MD-88 and even flew to some West Coast cities. I liked the glass displays, the navigation system, and even the autothrottles, which were more full authority than what we had on the Mad Dog.

I was quickly learning to appreciate the qualities of the different Boeing fleets. I only flew the -300 for one year and then Delta put out a big bid for the new fleet of B-737-800NG aircraft it was buying. Around this time, Delta decided that maintenance, spare parts, and training would save significant money if we only had fleets from one manufacturer. Except for the Mad Dog, Delta was going to operate an all-Boeing fleet! I bid the new -800 and prepared to learn all about Boeing's "Next Generation."

If I liked the -300G, I quickly learned to love the -800NG. It had so many things going for it. Yes, the cockpit was small and could be noisy, but the avionics were state of the art. Boeing was now looking at making it easy for a pilot to step from a 737 up to its bigger jets like the 767 and 777.

The cockpit glass displays consisted of six flat panels called the common display system (CDS). The autopilots, flight directors, and autothrottles were combined into the mode control panel (MCP). A synoptic panel could be called up for most major systems. Finally, the aircraft incorporated an amazingly precise heads-up display (HUD) for the captain. Once you learned Boeing's way of displaying and controlling information, you could later move up, as I did, to the B-767-400, and later the B-777-200, with significantly less effort because the logic of the automation was the same.

I particularly liked the HUD. In the simulator the instructor could set the ceiling and visibility to zero-zero, and you could hand-fly a precision ILS approach all the way to touchdown and complete the rollout to a stop. With the instructor setting you up completely blind in the sim, when the visibility was increased, you would see that you were still precisely on centerline. Amazing!

The aircraft was longer and heavier than the -300 I had just come from, holding 150 passengers, yet stopping distances were very short. One good example was Midway International Airport in Chicago. All the runways were 6,500 feet long or shorter, but because the airport was surrounded by buildings and other obstacles, the usable landing runways were cut back by at least a thousand feet. Not a problem for the -800. We consistently landed and turned off the runway after a rollout of only three thousand feet.

The -800 also had a much better range, allowing us to fly from Atlanta to the West Coast. I started to see a lot more of Los Angeles, Salt Lake City, Portland, and Seattle. We also flew extensively into the Caribbean, Central America, and even Caracas, Venezuela. I can look back now and remember fondly lying on the beach in Jamaica or poolside in Saint Lucia.

But it wasn't all fun and games. We stayed at a beautiful hotel in one Central American city where an American diplomat was kidnapped. Her saving grace was a locked door at the bottom of a stairwell, where they ended up leaving her bound and gagged! Also, in Caracas we stayed in an airport hotel because there were so many protests against the government, and highways were blocked between our original hotel and the airport. One crew had to arrange for a helicopter to take them from a nearby airport to the international airport! We enjoyed our flights and layovers, but you had to exercise caution.

I stayed on the -800 for six and a half years. I could have bid for the B-767, but we went to many of the same destinations and the pay was only ten dollars more per hour. I decided to stay where I was and enjoy a little seniority.

I also enjoyed the variety of flying in this category. Two of my first flights with a line-check airman were to Aruba and Central America. If you wanted to do coast-to-coast flights, you could bid on that. Getting bored? Bid Florida to New York the next month or Atlanta to San Juan. I found it interesting and never got bored with my schedule.

I also liked doing trips to New York since I grew up there. I would have layovers in Manhattan and plan to see a different part of the island with each visit. Rosann would come with me, and we would go to dinner and a Broadway show. I would jog through Central Park, visit the UN, or go down to Battery Park to see the Statue of Liberty.

When I came back from the desert after 9/11, I started flying the 737 again. On one New York layover I walked all the way downtown to the World Trade Center site. It was just a big empty hole in the ground by then. That by itself was sobering. What lifted my spirit that day was watching the New York Police Department hold a shift change at the site. They parked all their squad cars around it and conducted a briefing for the shift coming on duty. Who says New Yorkers don't have hearts?

The 737 would be the last narrow-body airliner I would fly. I really felt this was the airplane and the operation that seasoned me as a captain. I went everywhere in North and Central America, as well as the Caribbean. We did short out-and-backs to the big hub cities and flew coast to coast. I had dealt with medical emergencies, unruly passengers, difficult crew, and bad weather. I felt I was now ready for the big leagues.

CHAPTER 21

Big Boeings

I had held off bidding for the B-767-300 because the pay increase wasn't worth the loss of seniority. However, Delta and Continental had Boeing build a new version of the 767 to replace their retiring fleets of Lockheed L-1011s. Boeing built fifty B-767-400 aircraft split almost evenly between the two airlines. With every seat filled, Delta could put just over three hundred passengers and crew on these aircraft.

At first Delta used this new fleet for short runs from Atlanta to Orlando or coast-to-coast flights. However, the aircraft had been built for extended two-engine overwater operations (ETOPS). When a new marketing executive joined Delta, he changed that in a hurry. In short order we were flying all over the world. Common runs were Atlanta and New York to all over Europe, in addition to Atlanta to Hawaii, South America, and South Africa. This was terrific! I loved the long-range flights and seeing the rest of the world again.

My TOEs or transoceanic operating experience with a line-check airman were very interesting. The first one was to Europe and completely uneventful. The second one was going to be Salt Lake City to Maui. Delta deadheaded me to Salt Lake to meet my line-check airman the next morning. He had come in from LAX the night before and stopped to have breakfast somewhere before reporting for duty. Unfortunately, he got a very bad case of food poisoning that morning that did not become obvious until after we were airborne.

We were only a crew of two pilots since the flight would be less than eight hours long. About the time I was coasting out over San Francisco I was considering diverting south to LAX to replace the LCA. If his head wasn't buried in our trash bag, his tush was planted on a first-class toilet and stayed that way the whole way to Hawaii! He said he would be okay, but I flew the airplane, managed the navigation and flight logs, and made all the radio calls to ATC the entire way to Maui. After I landed and taxied to the gate, I looked at him and asked, "I passed, right?"

When we checked into the Maui Prince Hotel a short time later, he disappeared into his room, and we did not see him again until pickup time thirty-six hours later! In the meantime, the rest of the crew had great fun. We met by the beach with cocktails in hand to watch the sun go down over the Pacific, then had a nice dinner. The next morning, we all met up with rented fins and snorkels and walked down to a little cove where we spent the day snorkeling, observing multitudes of colorful fish, sea turtles, and coral. That was truly a beautiful and memorable trip, except of course for the LCA getting sick.

I only flew this fleet for two years, but the time was full of wonderful memories. We did two-man operations to Dublin and Shannon. I visited Trinity College and saw the Book of Kells, and I drank my share of Guinness. We flew to London and Manchester, where I learned to love Indian food and British ale. We visited pubs and restaurants all over Frankfurt, Munich, and Paris. I drank wine on the steps of the Sacré Coeur Basilica and enjoyed pints of beer in Germany, Spain, and England during the World Cup. Gosh, those Europeans love their soccer!

On my first trip to Rome, I walked to the Vatican and toured the Sistine Chapel and St. Peter's Basilica. I was very excited to think about being in such a holy place. St. Peter's tomb is directly below the high altar and there has been a church on this site since the time of Constantine the Great! As a practicing Catholic, it was an emotional moment.

I did a lot of trips to Lima, Peru, where we all raided the local Indian Market for handmade blankets and other souvenirs. São Paulo and Rio de Janeiro were lots of fun except for the tiring all-night flights back and forth to Atlanta and New York's JFK.

I really liked our flights from ATL to Honolulu. Because of the time zone difference, I always woke up early and went for a ten-mile round-trip hike from our hotel in Waikiki to Diamond Head and back. Then I would stop at a Cold Stone Creamery at the east end of Waikiki and treat myself. Just like during my time with the guard, I was fascinated by the large number of older people who would gather on the beach at those early hours to practice their tai chi. It was so beautiful to watch their graceful, flowing movements!

This was also the time I hooked Rosann on flavored Kona coffees. There was a little grocery store by our hotel that sold bags of coffee so cheap that they limited how many you could buy at a time!

Finally, no discussion about the 767-400 would be complete without talking about the trips to Johannesburg, South Africa. It is a thousand nautical miles farther from ATL to JNB than it is from ATL to Narita (NRT), Japan. Africa is a much bigger continent than most people realize. The 767 could not fly this 7,500-nautical-mile trip nonstop, so we always stopped in Dakar, Senegal, for twenty-four hours while another crew took our aircraft to the next arrival station.

The flight attendants would bring snacks and drinks from the airplane, and we would all meet poolside on the layover. Since there were always two crews, it was a sizable party every trip. For the most part it seemed that everyone behaved themselves. However, some of the crew, especially the male flight attendants, were living it up to the extreme. We stayed at a very nice hotel, but after I left the fleet, I heard that two crew members were caught in explicit activities at the pool late one night and Delta was asked to find somewhere else to stay. Too bad some adults just cannot seem to behave. More on that later.

Delta was the first US airline to offer direct flights from the US to Africa. As a place to enjoy top-rated safaris in parks like Kruger,

Johannesburg flights were nearly always full. On my first trip to JNB, my copilots wanted me to join them on a day trip to a nearby lion park. I had done many safaris in Kenya years before, so I politely declined. I figured if just one of those two copilots made it back to the hotel in one piece, then we could get the airplane back to Atlanta!

This local park fed a cow to the fenced lions once a week, and I'd heard the owner of the park had been mauled to death by his own lions. I figured the day *after* feeding would be safer than the day *before*! One of my copilots told me they make you sign a release, then drive you into the fenced park in an open-sided vehicle. The driver would drive a little way into the park, stop the vehicle, turn off the motor, then clap his hands together and say, "Come!" Then he would start the vehicle again and drive away quickly as the lions came out of the nearby bush. No thanks!

I saw one picture of a big lioness standing on the dirt road, looking intently at the departing vehicle holding my crew. I swear, if you made a poster of that picture, the perfect caption would be, HUMANS, THE OTHER RED MEAT!

I would have been happy to finish out the rest of my career on the 767-400 but I got greedy. A sizable bid came out that was offering positions on the B-777. I really wasn't senior enough to hold that category, but I thought, *what the heck, let me try for it*, and surprise, surprise, I got it! I was going to spend the last eleven years of my airline career flying the highest-paying and longest-range aircraft in the Delta fleet.

From the time I am writing this, it was seventeen years ago that I trained to fly the B-777 aircraft. At the same time, in January 2008, British Airways had a 777 crash just short of the London Heathrow Airport after a long flight from Beijing.

All jet fuel has a certain amount of water mixed in with it because of how fuel is stored after manufacture. This particular version of the 777 had Rolls-Royce engines that were susceptible to the engine's fuel-filter screens icing up after many hours at altitude where the fuel temperature could decrease to well below freezing. This would interrupt the fuel flow to the engine and cause the engine to "roll back."

At the end of my training on the 777, I asked the instructor to put the simulator at ten thousand feet over the Atlanta airport with a speed of 250 knots and fail both engines. It took me just a couple of tries to figure out the engine-out pattern to safely land the aircraft on the nearest runway. It may seem unusual to practice landing a half-million-pound glider, but if it was a possible scenario, I wanted to be ready. Thankfully, Rolls-Royce engineered a fix to that problem, and it has not reoccurred since.

I was very junior on the 777 in Atlanta for my first few years flying the fleet. We did flights to Mumbai, Dubai, Kuwait City, Lagos, Johannesburg, Seoul, Tokyo, Singapore, Sydney, and some of the major European cities. Being junior, I used to teasingly say I was Delta's "Africa Boy" because I did lots and lots of Lagos, Nigeria, and Johannesburg, South Africa. JNB is a nice layover, but many folks complained about Lagos (LOS) because Delta restricted us to the hotel complex for security reasons. We even had a sizable police escort to and from the airport.

Mumbai was a very exotic destination. However, it was sometimes more than eighteen hours to fly from JFK or ATL to BOM (Bombay—the city's name reverted to Mumbai in 1995). During my first layover there, I took a tour of the city. I saw Mahatma Gandhi's house, many of the city's districts, and several monuments. It really was a teaming mass of humanity!

Being the junior captain, I would typically fly the long trip home. These flights to and from Mumbai took all your physical and mental endurance to pace yourself for the duration. We each got two nearly four-hour breaks. Thank goodness I have no problem sleeping on the airplane. The flight would take off after midnight, as the cooler temperature gave the aircraft better performance. The -200LR (long range) version we flew on this trip has General Electric engines with 110,000 pounds of thrust each, can carry 320,000 pounds of fuel, and weighs 766,000 pounds on takeoff. However, the aircraft still rolled over a mile on takeoff and seemed to resist leaving Mother Earth.

Like many on this trip, I met a fellow who owned a leather shop named Aniel Bakhru. Aniel did good business servicing the different airline crews who laid over in Mumbai. He had a shop in the Oberoi Hotel where Northwest crews stayed. Delta crews stayed at the Taj Mahal Hotel. We then moved to the Leyland near the airport and later to a resort outside the city. Aniel would follow us each time to continue his service.

Delta eventually ended their service to Mumbai, so Aniel opened a shop across the street from the hotel we stayed at in Dubai, in the UAE. He would alternate being in the Dubai shop with his parents. I really loved his dad, Gopal. I would let them know I was coming to Dubai and Gopal would insist I come over the next day for lunch. They would order out Indian food that was to die for.

There was a terrorist attack in Mumbai in November 2008. I was scheduled to fly a BOM trip exactly one week after the attack. Both the Taj and Oberoi Hotels were attacked, and many people died but no flight crew, thank goodness! My flight, a week later, was the first Delta trip after the attack. We had two crews, twenty-six people, because one of our 777s was left at the airport when the layover crew was evacuated. I figured most of the crew would go to their rooms and lock their doors. I told them, "Get cleaned up and come down to the hotel bar. I will buy the first round or two." Would you believe all twenty-six people showed up for free drinks! About an hour or two later the bartender came up behind my right shoulder and whispered in my ear, "Captain, the bill is up to five hundred dollars. Should I cut them off?"

I responded, "Yeah, cut them off!" That's okay, because it was a good time and worth seeing everyone not go "slam click."

We did not service Kuwait City for very long, but I got to do a few of those trips as well. I remember one trip where our purser was a Coptic Christian originally from Cairo, Egypt. She worked in a hotel and met a US Navy officer who was working with the Egyptian military and kept asking her for a date. She told him he did not understand her culture. She said to him, "If you want to date me, you'll have to marry me." She said it took him two years, but he did finally marry her. They had three children, then divorced some years later.

As we were flying from ATL to KWI (Kuwait City), she came up to the cockpit for a break. She was telling us how the divorce rate in Egypt was very low, only 5 percent. I said, "Wait a minute. You mean one out of every twenty couples gets divorced? No wonder your men hate us Westerners!"

On the layover, she approached me and said a first-class passenger had asked her to go out to dinner. She insisted some of the crew had to come with them as chaperones. So, her date had about half a dozen of us as company that night. He took us to a nice traditional restaurant. What I did not know at that time was that the other captain and one of the other flight attendants had a "thing" going on. They were both married, just not to each other. They sat together, smoking flavored tobacco from water pipes and blowing hookah smoke at each other. I looked up to see many of the other patrons in the restaurant giving these two the evil eye because of their public display of attraction to each other, and Mohammed, our host, had eyes the size of saucers. I had to grab the captain and tell him to cool it before we all were taken out and stoned! Sometimes you can dress them up, but you can't take them out!

I also liked flying to our Asian destinations, but it can really be hard to sleep well when you are in a time zone that's twelve or thirteen hours different from back home. I found the only way to handle that was to develop a good routine. As an example, we would typically arrive in Narita, Japan, in the midafternoon. I would go to the hotel gym for a quick workout, clean up, then go to the hotel sports bar for a light meal and a beer. Usually by eight or nine I would be fast asleep.

Of course, I'd wake up at three in the morning, so I would fire up my laptop, answer emails, make calls back home, and generally take care of any business. By four or five I would be back in the hotel gym for a good hour-long workout. Then I would clean up and be at the hotel breakfast buffet by six. I loved that buffet because they had an endless selection of both American and Japanese fare. I am particularly partial to the Eastern diet, which is much lighter than our own. By eight I would be back in my room for a nice long nap. I would wake up around noon and leisurely pack up and get ready for our early-afternoon pickup. All in all, I found this kind of schedule easy and pleasant.

We also flew shorter trips out of Narita to Shanghai and Singapore with just a two-man crew. Shanghai was easy because the flight was only about three hours long and mostly during daylight. Singapore was much harder because the flight was just a bit under eight hours and at night, all while half a world of time zones away from home. Management finally put a third pilot on the Singapore flights and that made it much more bearable.

Shanghai was also a very interesting destination. It is a city of many contrasts. We would get in late in the evening and be back at the airport bright and early in the morning. Sometimes we would stay just a few minutes away at a very nice airport hotel, but most times we would take an hour-long ride to a truly grand hotel in downtown Pudong. It was such a long ride because the bus was electric and didn't drive much faster than fifty miles per hour!

Something I noticed at the airport hotel were these small flags ringing the lobby bar ceiling. Every country in the world was represented save one: Japan. Some things are never forgotten or forgiven.

On the outskirts of Shanghai, you see many small unadorned buildings where people live simple lives. Then you come downtown and see every kind of high-end shop, restaurant, and hotel. My room sometimes faced the Huangpu River, which winds its way through the downtown area. At night all the high-rise buildings were lit up with neon lights and the river was filled with numerous cruise and restaurant ships, again all festooned with neon lights of every color. It was truly an amazing sight! Of course, on many days the smog was so thick you could not see the opposite riverbank.

I did a few trips to Sydney out of Los Angeles. We would deadhead to LAX, then layover and leave the next day for SYD. Sydney is a pretty city with an old-world feel to it. It has nice people, good food, and beautiful vistas. The wharf was only a short walk from the hotel. I have taken the ferry tour around Sydney Harbour several times. You have beautiful views of the Sydney Opera House, Harbour Bridge, and Bondi Beach. We stopped at Bondi one day during a surfing competition. I had one of my pilots take a picture of me on the edge of the beach and I sent that picture to some friends. The message I got back told me to take a closer look past my right shoulder. I did not realize the girls could go topless! Better get my eyes checked.

I must include a discussion about Tel Aviv, Israel, because it was also a regular destination and an interesting place indeed. One of my first trips with a line-check airman after training on the 777 was to TLV. In fact, it snowed in Bethlehem that day. We stayed at the King David Hotel at that time. While a beautiful hotel, it was a little disconcerting to see profilers at the entry door, same as at entrances to the airport. These people are trained for two years to determine whether someone poses a threat, just by studying their face and behavior.

A ten-minute walk north, just off the beach, took us to a favorite little bar, run by a former lawyer from Chicago. If the story is to be believed, he escaped American justice—after being accused of involvement in the drug trade—by using his Israeli passport to come home, where he cannot be extradited. If he liked you, then he would take down a bottle of Maker's Mark for shots. I used to teasingly say that I have friends in low places, even overseas!

The flight home to ATL was an all-nighter. On one trip we were about a hundred miles east of the Azores when a flight attendant called the cockpit and said a passenger was having a heart attack. She made a request for a doctor on the passenger address system and had no less than six doctors respond, including the head of the cardiac unit at Emory University Hospital in Atlanta. We needed to land ASAP! It took us about twenty minutes to coordinate everything with Santa Maria Oceanic Control and Delta Air Lines, descend, dump eighty thousand pounds of fuel, and land.

We had to be sure to land under our maximum normal landing weight, otherwise we would not be able to depart until a qualified mechanic did an overweight inspection, and no such person existed at Lajes Field. With Lajes being 850 miles west of Portugal, we would have been there for at least twenty-four hours with nearly three hundred passengers and crew to accommodate.

It was three or four in the morning, and we literally woke up the whole airport. Thank goodness for the US Air Force. They have a contingent at Lajes that services many transient aircraft. I spent many nights there during my military days. Portuguese and US Air Force personnel met the aircraft and got the sick passenger off and to the hospital very quickly. I then went outside, we inspected the aircraft, and I showed the fueling personnel how to service a 777. Working from ATL, Delta flight operations was able to arrange our fuel, file a new flight plan, and dispatch us in about two hours. It's amazing how quickly the airline works when they need an aircraft in Atlanta for the next flight!

Again, I flew the 777 for eleven years and truly loved the aircraft. The cockpits had a host of modern displays that presented information in a way I found very easy to use efficiently. The model itself was more maneuverable than you would expect from something so big and heavy, and it was easy to consistently make good landings, especially since the radio altimeter announces your height above touchdown every ten feet starting at fifty feet.

Additionally, the airplanes were very dependable, especially considering their complexity. The 777 was designed with an electronic keel that has something like eighty different computers sending information back and forth. Honestly, the component most prone to failure was the passenger entertainment system. Our fleet of -200 ER (extended range) aircraft was the oldest, and we started to see more maintenance issues. The newer LR aircraft were my favorite with the more powerful GE engines. I was looking forward to the last few years of gallivanting all over the globe before the FAA forced me to give it up at age sixty-five.

Delta retired their fleet of eighteen B-777s shortly after all the COVID lockdowns. I was already retired, but even so, I was sorry to see the fleet go. I had some of my best years at Delta flying that fleet.

CHAPTER 22

Red Star Warbirds

When I retired from the military in 2002, I felt a little lost. I had been wearing a uniform since I was seventeen years old. It was at least partially how I defined my life and how I saw myself. One of my squadron mates, Alan Cockrell of Huntsville, Alabama, was a partner in a Russian Yak-52 aerobatic aircraft. The former Soviet countries used the Yak-52 as an aerobatic trainer for their DOSAAF personnel, a rough equivalent of the American Civil Air Patrol.

Early in 2002, Alan had invited me to come to Huntsville to fly the Yak with him. Rosann and I drove over on a Friday evening, and I spent the next two days discovering the joy of this kind of private flying. Alan and Gordy Sewell, a former USAF F-5 and F-4 pilot, reintroduced me to aerobatic and formation flying after a twelve-year hiatus on my part. By the end of Saturday, I was in the front seat of Alan's plane and flying tight formation on Gordy's wing!

One amusing memory was my first time taxiing from the front seat. The Yak uses an air-powered brake system with a bicycle-type grip on the control stick. I started the engine, performed my checklists, added power, displaced the rudder bars in the desired direction, and grabbed the brake handle. I promptly did a 360-degree turn, pivoting around the left main tire. That was *not* what I intended to do and, looking up, I saw everyone sitting in front of the airport FBO laughing their heads off! Let's try that again! I eventually got the hang of it.

Alan and Gordy flew out of Moontown Airport on a 2,200-foot grass runway. I quickly learned about path and speed control since we did not have the one- to two-mile-long runways available on military bases and at commercial airports. I was hooked. I immediately started looking for an airplane of my own.

In those first couple of weeks, I met BJ Kennamore and his son Brent. BJ had just recently bought a Chinese Nanchang CJ-6, a military trainer with very similar systems as the Yak-52. BJ and I really had an affinity for each other and quickly became close friends. He had bought his airplane from Mike McCoy, whose company in Chillicothe, Ohio, imported and restored many Nanchangs. Soon I was on my way to Ohio to see Mike's inventory.

Mike had quite a few aircraft that had not yet been restored. He also had a client's aircraft that was for sale at a very good price. After a demo flight with Mike, I made an offer on the client's aircraft and gave Mike a deposit check. When I got to the hotel that night, I called Alan to tell him about my planned purchase. He had previously shown me a Yak that his friend was selling, but the airplane was rough. This Nanchang was a really nice airplane.

Alan's reaction was very surprising. He was dead set against the Nanchang. He said it was underpowered, had seventy-five fewer horsepower than the Yak, and was not built as strong. He made it sound like such a bad choice that I immediately hung up and called Mike, asking him if I could back out of the deal. I felt terrible, but I did not want to make a seventy-thousand-dollar mistake.

I eventually found a Yak-52 in Columbus that had been specifically designed for the US market with US instrumentation and extended-range fuel tanks. It had very few hours in like-new condition. So, I made a deal for the Yak and planned to fly it down to Moontown. I got a late start that Friday, but it was a beautiful night flight. I arrived at Moontown with more fuel than Alan's aircraft could hold when full. When I told him that he said, "I hate you!"

This Yak would be a very quick education for me in aircraft

maintenance and insurance. It seemed the mechanic that serviced the aircraft before my departure had not properly inflated the landing-gear struts or tires. Three days later I was at BJ's private grass strip, Windward Pointe in Tuscumbia, Alabama. While taxiing out for takeoff, I went over a small depression from his driveway to the runway and the prop touched the ground, significantly damaging all three blades.

I contacted my insurance company, and they insisted that I send them copies of all my pilot information and the aircraft maintenance logbook entries to prove I had complied with my part of the insurance policy. They eventually paid for the engine inspection and a new set of propeller blades, minus a $2,500 deductible. They also eventually assigned blame to the previous mechanic but that did not lessen the pain of this expensive experience. I quickly learned that the owner is fully and solely responsible for not just himself but also for the airworthiness of the aircraft.

BJ and I spent that first year flying to every weekend fly-in breakfast and small-town air show we could find. He had never flown formation before, so I used my military background to teach him. I remember one Saturday when we flew all day long and I had to refuel twice. His low-fuel warning lights were just starting to blink during descent on the last leg. With flush riveting and a fully retracting landing gear, the Nanchang was twenty miles per hour faster than the Yak even though it had seventy-five fewer horsepower! Alan be damned, I was going to buy me a Nanchang!

I don't remember who told me, but I learned that there had been three brand-new Nanchangs imported into North America from the Hongdu factory in China. Two were bought by US customers and one was in Victoria, British Columbia. I visited Victoria Air Maintenance and quickly made a deal to buy the third airplane.

It took over six months to build up *Mongoose* as I wanted many modifications from the original design. I had Victoria add auxiliary fuel tanks, a landing-gear warning system, full instrument-capable avionics including autopilot and GPS, and a parking-brake system. I traveled to Victoria in November of 2002 to perform the test flights and ferry the aircraft home to Georgia. That was a very long trip, over two thousand nautical miles across the Cascade and Rocky Mountain ranges. It was a night sortie with less-than-clear weather the first day, in retrospect perhaps not the smartest thing to do in a single-engine piston airplane. But we made it home no problem, and I flew *Mongoose* 250 hours that first year.

While *Mongoose* was being built up, I advertised and sold my Yak-52. I trained the new owner, and when he finally left for home, I remember how strange it was to see my aircraft flying without me in it!

I owned *Mongoose* for twenty years and flew it for more than eleven hundred hours before selling it in 2023. I joined the Red Star Pilots Association (RPA) and flew at countless air shows and fly-ins around the country. I also typically attended a few RPA-sponsored events each year, where we taught others to fly formation and aerobatics. It is a wonderful community with lots of truly great people. The camaraderie is so strong that it feels like being back in the air force, where the shared risk of important missions made for very close personal bonds. Except for a handful of friends from my youth, I count these warbird brothers as my closest friends and confidants.

Along with being introduced to this warbird community and getting to make many new friends, I started considering buying some acreage on an airport and having a getaway home. BJ's Windward Pointe in Tuscumbia seemed ideal. So, I purchased 3.6 acres and spent a few years paying it off before finally building a six-thousand-square-foot hangar on the property.

I really enjoyed getting away to Alabama. I did not get over there nearly enough, but I tried to spend a day or two once or twice a month. It's an hour flight in *Mongoose*. I would taxi right up my driveway to the hangar door. We could fit three or four aircraft inside plus a couple of vehicles. The inside apartment had two bedrooms and was very comfortable. It was my man cave away from home. I sometimes teased the wife, "That's right, baby, kick me out of the house. I got someplace to go!"

Our Experimental Aircraft Association (EAA) group usually got together once a week for dinner, and nothing beat the pleasure of this very special group of friends. Additionally, I bought a 1967 Chevrolet Chevelle SS some years previously and put it through a full restoration. It was a very pretty car, and having it there was an excuse to get over to Windward every chance I could.

I finally sold my man cave in 2021 to Scottie Patterson, a good friend and fellow air force veteran, who lived in Muscle Shoals. It was time after twenty years. I hated parting with it, but I was keeping such a busy schedule that I couldn't get over there but once every few months. It's in good hands now.

This initial introduction to warbird flying opened many doors into other types of flying, but, over the years, I kept coming back to my roots. The people in Alabama and the fellow aviators in RPA have been the best community of friends and peers I have ever known.

On one occasion, I came back from a long weekend at a formation clinic in Waycross, Georgia, that we've done once or twice a year for nearly twenty years. The two dozen guys who always show up are such fun. We hail from many walks of life: former air force, navy, army, and marine aviators; civilian aviators; doctors, lawyers, businessmen; airline pilots. It reminded me that I had found a niche I could not imagine improving upon, and didn't intend to try.

CHAPTER 23

International Jets

In the mid-1990s, Rosann and I took a weeklong vacation in the North Carolina Blue Ridge Mountains one summer. We owned a time-share condominium in Colorado and traded for a week. We really fell in love with the area. We were in a town called Cashiers and not far from Highlands. We stopped at a real estate office and met Rowland Brazzeal and his wife Sherry. We ended up buying five acres in a beautifully secluded wooded area in Scaly Mountain, North Carolina. Scaly Mountain tops out around four thousand feet of elevation and is situated between Dillard, Georgia, and Highlands, North Carolina.

We took a loan to pay off the land, and I had hopes to someday live in the mountains, maybe even practice law there. We had a local architect design a beautiful house for us. The Rabun Gap-Nacoochee School was just fifteen minutes down the road, so I talked to my wife and daughters about moving up to the mountains and getting out of the big city. I was turned down flat! My idea of heaven did not suit my girls at all! I eventually paid off the land, and when it had doubled in value, I decided to sell it. Rowland did the honors, and I used the windfall to eventually buy two airplanes: a Yak-52 and a Cessna 172.

When I bought my two airplanes, I also started a little company named R&R Aviation to handle the testing, ferrying, and training flights I was starting to do more and more of. I eventually expanded my services to aircraft sales and insurance, and the company has consistently grossed six figures for many years.

I used the C-172 for rentals and flight instruction. One day a student and I flew over to Gadsden, Alabama. I had heard about a company there named International Jets (IJ) that did maintenance on jet warbirds, particularly the Czech-built Aero Vodochody L-39 Albatros. A beautiful trainer and ground-attack aircraft, I honestly never thought I would have an opportunity to fly the L-39, but I still wanted to see the airplanes up close.

The owner of IJ was Joe Brand, a young mechanic in his late thirties. Joe worked for Rudy Beaver, a much older local businessman, who saw an opportunity to make money bringing in L-39s and other types of former Soviet equipment after the USSR broke apart. Rudy eventually sold the company to Joe and his wife. I had a nice visit with Joe that first day at IJ, but I didn't really expect anything to come of it.

I had been flying Yaks and Nanchangs and had the pleasure of flying in a few L-29 Delfíns that some friends in Florida owned. The L-29 was the predecessor of the L-39. It was not as pretty and not as fast, but it burned the same amount of fuel. I called it the "Soviet Tweet" because it had almost identical flight characteristics as the T-37 I instructed in for three years in the air force.

While flying the Yaks and Nanchangs, I met an Atlanta businessman named Jay Land and his son Alex. Jay owned a Nanchang, and we flew together quite a bit as I was teaching them to fly formation. It was Jay and I that got to fly the L-29s with our Florida friends. I remember telling Jay, "The L-29 is fun, but the cat's meow is the L-39. You should buy one." A month later Jay called me, and that is exactly what he had done. Now he insisted we work together to get our rating.

We went to Pride Aircraft in Rockford, Illinois, for ground school. We then went to IJ in Alabama for flight training with a former Ukrainian squadron commander named George. I had one flight in the back seat, then one flight in the front seat. George signed me off for solo and I proceeded to teach myself the airplane. Jay and I flew his aircraft to St. Mary's in southeast Georgia to get our recommendation ride from Zach McNeil, an active-duty navy helicopter pilot and L-29 owner. Doug Gilliss flew out from California to give us our check rides, and we flew home to Atlanta as newly minted jet warbird pilots!

Only a few short weeks later I got a phone call out of the blue from Joe Brand at IJ. It seemed their instructor pilot George had gone home to Ukraine, and their other instructor got hired by a cargo outfit. Joe asked if I could start training their customers. The rating in the L-39 had cost me five thousand dollars, and I was very concerned about spending that kind of money because I didn't think it would ever pay off. Boy was I wrong! In for a penny, in for a pound—I answered "sure" and started working for IJ right away as a contract instructor.

Each new jet owner required about one to two weeks for ground and flight training, and I remember training thirteen pilots for their rating that first year. In fact, I once calculated that IJ accounted for 75 percent of R&R Aviation's revenue. I quickly became a very busy instructor, juggling my time between IJ, Delta Air Lines, and family. But I must admit I really enjoyed flying the jet warbirds. I even expanded my ratings to include the L-29, British Provost, and US/Canadian T-33.

In the fall of 2005 IJ had a huge warbird gathering called a "Jet Blast." We must have had nearly two dozen L-39s at Gadsden. It was great fun flying as an instructor pilot (IP) for what were mostly civilian pilots with no military background. I had joined the Classic Jet Aircraft Association (CJAA), and Jay and I flew all over the US to attend their sponsored fly-ins and annual convention.

Two things came out of that 2005 fly-in in Gadsden: I found out that Joe Brand was beginning to suffer a serious medical decline from the ravages of diabetes, and I got a phone call that my dear friend BJ lost his only son. In fact, I left Gadsden the same day that call came and drove immediately to Huntsville, where BJ's son had been flown by helicopter to a medical center.

BJ and Charlotte were devastated to say the least. To this day the loss of their only child is written all over Charlotte's face, and while my former marine buddy soldiers on, we talk about the depth of a pain that will never end. Life is fragile, and so is our hold on a peaceful existence in the face of life's tragedies. In the worst case, life sucks you dry. In the best case, it fills you up as you draw closer to those who truly love you.

Back at IJ, Joe's wife tried her best to run the company without Joe. His kidneys and eyes were failing, and it was difficult for him to spend any time at the shop when his medicine never seemed to keep his body properly regulated. It reminded me of my stepfather Frank's condition years before. Joe died of his disease only a few months after that fall gathering. I remember speaking at his funeral and doing a flyby at his grave site.

For the next year I did everything I could to help his wife, but her heart just wasn't in it. She had some really good staff, but she also had two young children at home and needed money to run the household. IJ began a death spiral I feared would not end until the company was out of business. In fact, that very nearly happened.

A businessman client from New Hampshire tried twice to buy IJ from Joe's wife, but he could simply never make a deal with her. When I realized just how much IJ contributed to R&R Aviation's income, I started thinking about how I might be able to make a deal to buy the company.

Another good friend of mine was a Yak owner and a former marine F/A-18 pilot. David McGirt lived in Atlanta, and we became acquainted through the RPA. David was working for a European investor at the time and had become something of an expert at buying failing companies, turning them around, and then selling them at a profit. We were at a flying event when I pulled David aside and presented the situation about IJ, asking for his guidance.

David listened patiently then mapped out a phased buyout plan that would only require fifty thousand dollars up front. This was something I could afford to do, so I made an offer to Joe's wife. Like Bob, I found her very difficult to negotiate with and we almost did not make the deal. In the end, though, I made a take-it-or-leave-it offer that her attorney highly recommended she accept. Finally, on May 1, 2007, I became the proud but naive owner of International Jets in Gadsden, Alabama. What I did not know about business could fill volumes, but boy was I about to learn everything in a hurry. Talk about drinking from a fire hose!

When I first took over IJ, we didn't have a single airplane scheduled to be in the shop that month. I immediately started phoning clients and working to get business in. I got one Florida client to commit two of his jets and things started to pick up after that.

I knew I was never going to become wealthy running IJ, but we managed to keep our heads above water for nine years. Just about all our customers were wealthy men who had a passion for aviation. While they made very good money in their chosen field of expertise, they guarded their own wallets jealously. Being frugal is one thing. Being stingy is another! To this day a car dealership maintenance shop charges more per hour than our market could ever bear.

Our technician team was a very interesting menagerie of civilian and former-military technicians. Some of them hailed from East Germany, Ukraine, the Czech Republic, and Slovakia. A few years later, when we started doing military contracts in Africa, we added technicians from England, France, and Botswana. At our zenith I had thirty-two employees.

Everything was a struggle in the beginning. It never ceased to amaze me how the company lived payroll to payroll, always having just enough to pay the bills, and not much left over. However, I managed to turn the company around that first year, and we closed out with a rise in gross income and enough to pay a small Christmas bonus. I was heartened.

Our business is purely discretionary. That is to say, the jet warbirds we worked on were not necessities, but rather luxuries. Many of our clients owned multimillion-dollar business jets, yet they would fight us tooth and nail for every dime we charged them for our services. Also, the Thanksgiving and Christmas holidays always resulted in a couple of very slow months as our clients focused their energies on family and flew their airplanes less. That time of year always stressed me out because I hated telling a good worker that I was going to have to fire him or lay him off.

There were so many issues to deal with: pushy clients, parts shortages, and cultural differences between employees from different countries. On top of these issues, Joe's wife had remarried, and her new husband seemed to convince her I had not paid her enough for the business. So, she sued us. It took three years and tens of thousands of dollars before the court finally ruled in our favor.

About six months after I bought IJ, and before she sued us, I managed to bring on three new business partners. Each of them was an L-39 owner, a client, and a successful businessman, and each had a vested interest in seeing IJ flourish, even if only for their own purposes. I made a deal with each, and we bought out Joe's wife. We were now four equal partners with me wearing all the important hats: president, CEO, CFO, COO. That worked in the beginning but proved problematic years later.

One of the functions we really needed to fix was our ability to account for inventory and keep a steady supply of new spare parts flowing into IJ. We were maintaining about four dozen L-39s each year, plus doing a couple of in-depth restorations, and selling parts to others around the country and overseas.

My East German technician brought many parts with him from home, but his prices were not cheap, and I felt it was a conflict of interest to buy from him. Igor from Slovakia also sourced parts for us from his home country, but Igor was always easier to deal with and fairer in his pricing. Lastly, we bought many parts from a former Soviet instructor pilot from Ukraine. Mikhail lived in Gadsden and sourced many parts from factories back home.

Mikhail saw an opportunity with IJ and tried to arrange a joint venture to, in essence, become our parts department. I got a lot of pushback on that idea from my technicians. They did not trust Mikhail and thought the parts he provided were sometimes not of the best quality or did not come with the appropriate paperwork.

Then something amazing happened. I got a call out of the blue from the Nigerian embassy. Their air force was looking for L-39 parts. They sent me a list and Mikhail and I priced it. Then they sent me an expanded list. We priced that. Finally, I got a call, and they asked us to come to DC for a meeting with their defense attaché. So, we flew to DC and had a nice meeting with their military representatives. Shortly thereafter we were invited to travel to Nigeria to assess the NAF's L-39 operation in Kano.

Mikhail and I were quite excited. We could see this becoming a multimillion-dollar contract that would far exceed our current level of income. I brought an airframe technician and Mikhail arranged for an engine expert from the Motor Sich factory in Zaporizhzhia, Ukraine, to accompany us. We all met in Lagos, Nigeria, and the NAF arranged for a Dornier 228 twin turboprop to fly us to air force headquarters in the capital, Abuja.

On the way to Abuja, the aircraft commander told me we would be making a stop in Benin City. It seemed the minister of defense and his entourage were stuck there with a broken airplane. The minister and five others boarded the flight, and he sat across from me. After staring at our four white faces for ten minutes, the minister asked bluntly, "What are you doing here?" I told him of our mission, and he had no further comment.

In Abuja we were taken to the Chelsea Hotel, just two blocks away from NAF headquarters. It was a pretty nice hotel with its own swimming pool, tennis court, restaurant, and bar. I was given a large suite of rooms and was looking forward to meeting the general staff at HQ the next morning.

My sponsor for this visit was none other than their number two-man, Air Vice Marshal Anene Okafor, the air officer for operations. In a huge conference room, Okafor's staff explained what they wanted my team to do. We were to travel to Kano, where they flew the L-39 as their advanced pilot-training aircraft. They had bought twenty-four of these airframes in the mid-eighties, but only a handful were still flying. The next day we boarded the Dornier 228 and flew to Kano.

I would like to digress here for a moment. Anene is Igbo, from eastern Nigeria. If you remember your history, the country suffered a civil war from 1967 to 1970 when the Igbo people tried to form their own country after years of brutal discrimination. I remember charities raising money for the starving children of Biafra at that time. I once asked Anene what it was like back then and how he felt about it. He told me very seriously there were things you just had to forget so you could move on with your life. Wise words that so many people have great difficulty following.

Nigeria is very close to the equator and so is generally very hot and humid. However, the northern part of the country is quite arid and desert-like. It was not uncommon to experience daytime highs of 110 or hotter. It certainly is enough to sap your energy and dehydrate you in days. However, it surprised me to see the local technicians arrive at work in the morning with jackets on. Even eighty degrees seemed cool to them.

We spent a week doing a complete assessment of every facet of Kano's operation. We looked at spare parts inventory, warehousing, pilot training and facilities, technician training, aircraft and engine condition, and logbooks. NAF's twenty-four L-39ZAs had been overhauled once in a Belarus facility in the late nineties. Three aircraft had crashed and another three had been landed gear up. So, there were eighteen airframes that could conceivably be returned to service.

One night the chief of the maintenance squadron, Sunny Makinde, took us downtown to a little watering hole called the French Café. It was a nice place with a restaurant, bar, and little lounge area. Sunny had some friends from the local university join us and we had a very pleasant night of drinking and socializing. I remember looking over at one point and seeing a guy who looked like he was from the Middle East giving us the evil eye. I glanced at our security guy, and he was watching this fellow like a hawk. Reminded me of a Clint Eastwood line in one of his *Dirty Harry* movies, telling the bad guy, "Go ahead, make my day!"

As we were leaving that night I stopped in the bathroom and ran into another American. This surprised me because we were five thousand miles from home and off the beaten track. The next day I was interviewing the flight-training squadron commander and telling him about my encounter. He said, "Oh, that's a friend of mine. He married an African girl." He called the guy and confirmed it was him. It is a small world, even when far across the globe in Africa!

After a week in Kano, we returned to Abuja to brief the headquarters staff on our findings and to make a proposal. Mikhail wanted to stretch out the high cost of returning so many aircraft to service over six years. I wanted to create a pan-African pilot training program much like the USAF ENJJPT program I instructed at in Texas years before. It would have been a one-hundred-million-dollar program that would have been cash-flow positive in three years and paid for itself in six. Unfortunately, NAF did not have the funding or mindset to enact such a program, so they only approved a fraction of our plan.

It took most of calendar year 2010 to negotiate, approve, and sign the contract with the Nigerian Ministry of Defence. This was a precursor of many difficulties to come. Mikhail was becoming very hard to deal with. This was supposed to be a joint venture. I wanted to make use of his expertise and sourcing of spare parts, technicians, and overhaul services, but he increasingly tried to take over every aspect of the contract, even though my company was responsible for its performance.

I started doing my own research into establishing contracts and arrangements for these services in the former Eastern Bloc. What I learned was that IJ was being overcharged for parts and overhaul services. Finally, Nigeria was ready to transfer our first payment. We had to provide an advance-payment guarantee through a bank. The bank required my partners and I to give personal guarantees. I asked Mikhail, as a partner in this project, to also give a personal guarantee. He refused.

My partners and I discussed the circumstances with our lawyer and decided to end the joint venture and return to dealing with Mikhail as a normal, outside vendor. At one point we were so fed up with the situation that we offered to pay him to go away. He wanted all his money up front. We could not afford to do that and simultaneously fulfill the contract. The result was Mikhail suing IJ.

At the time I was writing this part of my memoir, the lawsuit was still pending. It had been a stupendous waste of time, effort, and money. We spent as much money as we would have if Mikhail had accepted our staggered-payment offer, to be paid out as we received milestone payments ourselves. The use of the American judicial system as a weapon has truly turned my stomach. Facts and fairness have had nothing to do with both lawsuits I faced. It is all about threatening another until they pay you to go away. The reality is that our tort system is abused and does the term "justice system" a severe disservice.

CHAPTER 24

Nigeria

I have been doing work for the Nigerian Air Force for fifteen years, and it has been the most challenging environment to do business and retain my sanity. However, it has also been some of the most satisfying work I have done as an owner of IJ. Over the years NAF has used our technicians to help maintain their fleets of L-39s, Alpha Jets, C-130s, and Agusta helicopters. I have had large metal hangars built for them in the US and shipped to Nigeria. I have trained their instructors and student pilots in trainer and fighter aircraft. We have provided spare parts. The work is never-ending and there seems to be a constant need for outside services. On top of that, their system is incredibly difficult to work with.

Our first contract was supposed to be finished in twelve months. I realistically figured it would take twenty-four months to complete the project, bringing six L-39s back to flight status. But it took over six years, mostly due to extensive payment delays. This is a bureaucracy like I had never seen before. No one steps beyond their limited area of responsibility, and everyone expects a little "motivation" to do their job, otherwise paperwork is delayed or even "lost."

I was impressed that NAF always seemed to come back to us because they knew we were honest and competent. We always got our work done correctly. It was just so hard to get paid! One contract had to be accomplished in their local currency, naira. Because of official currency-exchange regulations, to pay for the European facilities doing overhaul work, my Nigerian bank had to use the black market to exchange naira into dollars. That cost me 10 percent of the money paid and made it a break-even contract at best.

The second contract was to put their fleet of Alpha Jet ground-attack fighters back in service. NAF had retired the fleet a few years before due to unwillingness to pay expensive European contractors and an inability to keep the fleet flying themselves. We put nine of eleven aircraft back in service over a three-year period. Two more aircraft were cannibalized of spare parts to such an extent that it would have been nearly impossible to put them back in service. The balance of the twenty-four aircraft originally purchased in the 1980s had either been crashed or damaged in gear-up landings.

The Alpha Jets were based in Kainji in the western part of the country, near the Kainji Reservoir on the Niger River. The hydroelectric facility provides most of the electricity for the whole country. However, the military base always seemed to be the first to lose power, and for at least a few hours every day. We shipped portable generators to Kainji so our technicians could continue to work. I must give Mike Lee and Jonathan McCormick great credit. Mike ran the technical program to reconstitute the fleet, and Jon Boy did a brilliant job building a temporary paint booth to paint the airplanes as they were brought back into service.

When we first started working in Kainji in 2011, the air base was basically in mothball status. The Alpha Jets had not been flown for about five years. The base's roads were badly pockmarked. The runway needed to be repaired. The VOR (local navigation station) was out of service, and there were no runway lights for night operations.

When I did all the test flights on the first three aircraft, we would take off, fly to the dam on the south end of the Kainji Reservoir, climb up, do the test profile over the reservoir, keep the reservoir constantly in sight, descend back over the dam, fly three miles southwest to pick up a visual on the town and the air base, and land. Do not lose sight of the reservoir! Eventually we bought handheld GPS receivers and mounted them in the front cockpit.

Once we had the Alpha Jets flying again, we modified one end of a huge hangar into a makeshift paint booth. We painted four of the aircraft in a NATO two-tone gray. They came out of the paint booth looking like new, but the Nigerians did not like the scheme. They said it was too difficult to see, as though that wasn't the point of camouflage! So, we painted the rest of the aircraft in the original NAF green-and-tan camouflage scheme with the sky-blue belly. These also came out looking great, just more visible.

As a former USAF fighter pilot, I would have preferred something more concealed since the Alpha Jet performs its mission at low level and would be susceptible to ground fire. In fact, a few years later several of their Alpha Jets would be shot down by Boko Haram while flying low-level sorties in the north of the country. This Islamist terrorist group later executed one of the pilots by cutting off his head on camera. This was a sobering reminder that this work and its risks were for keeps.

In 2012 and 2013 the NAF was involved in the French operation in nearby Mali. The NAF sent some of their Alpha Jets to a forward-operating location in Niamey in the southwest of Niger. The Nigerians set up a low-level route to the north of the city for aircrew training when not on combat missions. During one of those low-level training missions, one of the Alpha Jets crashed. IJ had a vested interest in this accident because we had placed this aircraft back in service, so we were invited to participate in the investigation.

NAF did a very thorough and professional job laying out the details of the crash scene. Mike Lee and I traveled to headquarters in Abuja and reviewed all the evidence. It turned out the low level had some very large turns over featureless, semidesert terrain. The trees in this area were quite stunted, giving the flight crew a false sense of height when in fact they were very close to the ground.

On one particularly sharp turn, the aircraft clipped a tree and then crashed, leaving a few-thousand-foot-long debris field. The pictures of the wreckage showed that some of the ejection-seat components that should have stayed in the aircraft were found outside with the seats, which had been forcibly ejected from the aircraft upon ground contact. We were certainly sorry for the loss of life and the aircraft, yet at the same time relieved our work had not contributed to the loss.

In the spring of 2014, a contingent of NAF operations and multiple engineering officers traveled to the US. They were looking at several airplanes and equipment vendors to make purchases. They visited IJ, and while I did not participate in the sale, NAF eventually bought four former German Air Force (GAF) Alpha Jets that had been imported after their retirement from the GAF. Hans Vanderhoffen in Arlington, Washington, purchased about two dozen of these aircraft, and Mike Lee assembled and made them airworthy. About half of this fleet ended up in Canada. Discovery Air Defence operates their fleet on military contracts to this day. The other half were sold to American individuals as warbirds, and the rest were operated by AirUSA on military contracts.

Initially the two sellers of the four aircraft were supposed to provide ferry pilots to fly them the seven thousand nautical miles to Nigeria. While the Alpha Jet with drop tanks has a one-thousand-nautical-mile range, this is still a very long, arduous journey across the North Atlantic Ocean and the Sahara Desert. The risks are real and considerable.

After the sale of the four aircraft, the sellers declined the offer to ferry the jets. And upon asking around, the Nigerian attaché was told to contact yours truly, as I was one of the few people in the US with the experience to safely ferry their airplanes. Aminu Yakuba contacted me in January 2015, and a contract was quickly signed. I have now ferried thirteen military trainer and fighter aircraft to Africa, Europe, and South America. I have also ferried dozens of jet and piston warbirds all over North America. Some of these trips are newsworthy by themselves, and I have written many articles for domestic and international magazines. I will have many stories to tell about these trips in another chapter.

Our work in Nigeria has been an incredible education and experience. After twenty-eight years in the USAF and ANG, I feel as if my career was extended by the projects we took on for the NAF. At one point I had a dozen technicians from Europe and America working on four distinct fleets of airplanes and helicopters at four different air bases around the country. I had briefed the general staff at NAF headquarters. I had had serious discussions with their minister of defense. All of this is above and beyond anything I could have imagined before I received that first fateful phone call.

I only have one regret after fifteen years of faithful service to the NAF. As I said in the beginning, it is a very difficult place to work. Try to imagine a country the size of Texas, with 150 million residents living on an average of two dollars a day. Imagine a country pieced together half a century ago by a colonial power more worried about what another colonial power was doing than about the impact of forcing such disparate tribes as the Hausa, Igbo, and Yoruba peoples to live as one. In fact, the Nigerian Islamist terrorist organization's name, Boko Haram, comes from the Hausa language and literally translates to "Western learning is forbidden." Boko Haram has killed more people and displaced more refugees than any other Islamist terror group!

In all this complexity it is human nature to strive to take care of oneself whenever possible. My personal thinking is: If you do not have faith in the future, then you try to take all you can today. The Nigerian economy is very corrupt, and that corruption invades every facet of their lives, to include those in uniform. Don't misunderstand me. I have made many friends in Nigeria, and I have seen true patriots, courageous men who put themselves at risk for a chance to accomplish great things. Unfortunately, I have also seen some senior leaders, both in and out of the military, who will stop at nothing to line their own pocket and destroy anyone who gets in their way. We often found ourselves trying to resolve a delayed payment, delayed for months by such people through misinformation and interference. It is a sobering environment that can daunt even the hardiest of souls. I continue to hope I will be able to serve the needs of the NAF in the future. They certainly need outside services. However, if I was totally honest with myself, I would admit I liked this work because of how it made me feel about me—that I was needed for something truly important: saving lives!

By early 2013, I had gone through several directors of maintenance from when I first bought IJ in 2007. It's a hard job with a lot of responsibility in both the office and on the shop floor. Paperwork, logbooks, and invoices must be meticulously created. Vendors must be continuously sourced for needed parts, equipment, and services. Technicians need to be supervised for maintaining standards of performance, and the different shops (maintenance, parts, avionics, and paint) need precise coordination to keep projects on schedule. It can be a persistently stressful job with little relief in sight.

We had one technician from the shop who worked hard and was honest as anyone can be, but the stress started to get to him. Before him, we hired an outside person with great experience, to include being a lead mechanic at a major airline. Unfortunately, he was sloppy in his work and presented me with personal problems that could not be ignored. He even tried to turn my partners against my involvement. I finally gave him the opportunity to walk away before I fired him.

My own technician stepped up next and did a good job, but it overwhelmed him. I saw that I was going to need someone else in the position soon, and, finally, another one of my technicians took on the role. He was a former USAF mechanic, so I hired him as our parts-department manager and moved him onto the shop floor, where he worked on L-39s and other aircraft projects. One day he approached me and offered to take over as director of maintenance.

The old chief was relieved to go back to turning wrenches, and our new chief seemed to be an intelligent and well-organized manager. I liked having someone I could trust to run the day-to-day activities, but I wanted to stay involved. We butted heads many times. He wanted to go about his responsibilities, and for me to stay fully hands-off. I appreciated his feelings but felt a financial obligation to my partners to stay intimately involved.

Beyond the friction between us, he did relay to me more than once that he was feeling the stress of the position. I finally gave in and hired a former US Navy navigator and weapons-systems officer to cover the administrative duties so that the chief could concentrate on the mechanical work. I later heard from other employees that the two of them would sit in the office and bad-mouth me. I'm sure I gave them plenty to complain about, but it didn't seem like professional behavior, and being typically Southern, most of my other employees just kept their heads down and their mouths shut. It wasn't until I fired the admin fellow, and the chief quit, that the others finally told me what had been going on.

It all started in 2013 while in Nigeria for meetings at NAF headquarters. As I sat in a Lagos hotel waiting for my flight home later that night, I called the shop to relay some information about my meetings. I was asked if I had told the maintenance chief yet, and I said it was next on my to-do list. I had already talked to my contacts at NAF and figured it could wait. I got home that weekend and went to the shop Monday morning, but the chief never showed up for work. He was offended that I had not talked to him first, but I think it was just an excuse to leave all the stress behind. Of course, leaving without any advance notice really put us in a bind.

About the same time that the chief of maintenance left us, my Slovak technician gave us his two-week notice. He was tired of living in small-town Alabama and said he wanted a "different view outside his window." I offered him more money and even the director of maintenance position, but he had already made up his mind.

We had been working on an Ilyushin aircraft project in Michigan. My lead mechanic there was from Oklahoma but willing to travel, so I offered him the director of maintenance job in Alabama. My partners called a meeting and decided that we would hire him, he would get free rein of the domestic operation, and I would restrict myself to the international and military operations. While this would decrease my workload and stress, I also felt like I was being shunted aside. I did not like it at all, and hiring him would indeed prove to be a mistake.

He only lasted about eight months. He, like others, tried to turn my partners against me, all while running the shop with an iron fist. He would threaten employees with their job if they did not do what he wanted without question. He hired untrained technicians who damaged customers' airplanes, eventually costing us tens of thousands of dollars to avoid lawsuits. He dropped an aircraft wing and then lied about it happening in shipment to IJ. Finally, one of my employees spoke up about some other issues. I finally convinced my partners that we should fire this chief of maintenance.

Looking back now, the first chief of maintenance who left without notice started a chain reaction that would ultimately lead to IJ's demise. Only one mechanic had the courtesy to give us notice. Most were so argumentative with Uli, my former East German technician, that Uli finally left IJ to work for a competitor upon receiving his green card.

Of course, those that left had no issue calling every one of IJ's clients and offering their services at a lower price, telling them how IJ was in crisis. Customers jumped ship without a second thought. I have made dozens of friends in the warbird community, but there is no loyalty in the service end of things. Even legal action to stop these former employees would have been a waste of time and money, since they had nothing to pay off a judgment if we won.

I held the company together for another four years, struggling to keep costs down and bring in any revenue I could find. Finally, in the fall of 2016, I sold our domestic assets to a competitor and closed the business in the spring of 2017. It had been a ten-year roller-coaster ride, and I was getting out with basically no debt. I cannot emphasize enough what a relief it was to finally get that monkey off my back.

In the meantime, I started a new company with a handful of engine technicians and made a deal with the Ukrainian design bureau, SE Progress, to do in-depth repair and overhaul of the AI-25TL engines in the L-39. We have made tremendous progress in ten years of development and can now repair or overhaul these jet engines. With 260 L-39s in the US and no one else in the States with this capability or expertise, I am excited to do this needed work. Of course, I get to do all the test flying, which I truly love. Some might think that's a little crazy. Maybe I am!

CHAPTER 25

Over the Ocean and Through the Wastes

Being a risk-taker is relative. What counts as a risk? How about calculated risks? Is it taking a risk if it is something you are intimately knowledgeable about and you can do much to mitigate the threat? I will be the first to admit that I love a challenge, and there is nothing more satisfying than doing something difficult, something almost no one else has done. Ferrying fighter and trainer aircraft from North America to Europe, Africa, and South America over the last fifteen years seems to have been my holy grail of risk-taking. You've heard the expression, "Never make the same mistake twice"? Well, I've done it thirteen times, three of those times solo!

In January 2010, International Jets had a visit from an Italian businessman and pilot named Gianluca. To this day "G" is a great friend. He had been thinking about buying an L-39 for a long time and finally decided to do something about it. G bought two aircraft from IJ, and I even arranged for his aircraft to work on military contracts in Europe a few years later.

Gianluca came to the US with his financial manager, David. They toured the shop and looked over the aircraft I had for sale, finally settling on an aircraft that a widow was selling. We did a full restoration and a very fancy paint job that was designed by Mirco Pecorari. It turns out Mirco lived only eighty kilometers from G! Small world. Worth mentioning is the fact that my wife, and her mom who lived with us, are Sicilian and wonderful cooks. Gianluca and David stayed with us in our home, and they ate like kings for the week!

We received permission to export the aircraft, and I planned for a June departure, estimating a four-day trip from Gadsden, Alabama, to Fano, Italy, on the Adriatic Coast. What worried me was an active volcano in Iceland that was wreaking havoc on air traffic across the Atlantic Ocean and in Europe. Eyjafjallajökull did not stop its eruptions until two weeks before my scheduled departure. In fact, the same volcano erupted again the following spring and came within two weeks of disrupting another ferry flight!

These trips across the oceans, jungles, and deserts have plenty of dangers, some of which you can prepare for and some of which you cannot. Even in the middle of summer, the North Atlantic Ocean surface temperature is only about eight degrees Celsius. You are hundreds of miles from any rescue vessel in a single-engine aircraft and can only carry the most basic survival equipment in these fighter cockpits.

With an L-39 Albatros, external fuel tanks increase the range from about 500 to 700 nautical miles, plus reserves. The longest leg of the journey was on day two from Goose Bay, Canada, to Narsarsuaq, Greenland—675 nm. On my first trip, ATC routed me slightly less than direct due to conflicting traffic. The leg was now 713 nm to an airport with a single runway, and the nearest paved alternate airport was over 400 nm away. I arrived in Greenland with ninety gallons of fuel, exactly forty-five minutes of reserve. Also, even though it was June, and I expected good weather, I still had to fly an instrument approach on five of the first six legs of the journey.

During this first trip, I flew the aircraft solo to Scotland because I did not want the responsibility of another crew member. Also, G's wife Georgia told him, "If Richard can get the airplane safely to Scotland, then I'm okay with you flying with him the rest of the way to Italy." G was waiting for me when I arrived in Wick, Scotland.

I had rented my survival equipment from Andrew Bruce of Far North Aviation. He would pre-position equipment at Goose Bay,

Labrador, and customers could drop it off as they crossed going east or west. The equipment included a raft, a personal locator beacon, a survival suit, and a life preserver. Later I would buy all my own equipment. The first time I used the survival suit was in Goose Bay and it made me look like Gumby. My gloved fingers were so fat that every time I selected a button on the GPS, I pushed three at once. I finally had to strip the suit to the waist and pray that I would have time to suit up if I had to ditch in the ocean!

Andrew Bruce at Far North is a truly interesting fellow. He is extremely helpful, even to the point of being humorously distracting from the goal at hand. He once canceled a flight plan my handler back in Canada had filed for me and filed a completely different route to my next stop, Liège, Belgium. The amazing part is that Andrew was completely correct. He routed me east to the North Sea and then south to the Low Countries and it was much more efficient!

On another ferry of an L-39 to Europe, a perfect storm of three low-pressure weather systems converged around northern Scotland. There was a significant headwind at altitude and the surface winds on arrival were forty to fifty knots right down the runway. I landed safely and taxied to the old WWII hangar, where Andrew simply threw the doors open and taxied me straight inside. My God did that wind sound eerie as it howled around the eves of that old WWII building. That night I stayed at Mackay's Hotel, another ancient structure. The vibrating skylights in my top-floor room moaned a devilish serenade all night long as the wind whipped around them.

Another time we had to stay in Iceland for three days because of severe fog in the UK. This was the summer of 2012 when England was hosting the Olympics. We finally received a good weather forecast for our arrival time in Wick, Scotland. Of course, it was just a forecast. A hundred miles from the destination, I called Andrew on our VHF radio and asked about the weather. To this day his response makes me laugh, as it so describes his personality. "Richard, I cannae see mah hand in front of me face!"

Anyway, on the long trip from Alabama to Italy, I had never landed a jet on grass before, and Fano was a 3,900-foot turf runway. We handled it fine, but with trees and power lines at either end, the actual usable runway was quite a bit shorter. You had to be very sure about following your short-field procedures. G put me up in a hotel right on the beach, and my wife Rosann flew Delta to Rome. G sent a retired policeman to pick her up and drive her to the east coast. For the next two weeks Rosann laid on the beach every day while I rode a Vespa motor scooter to the airport to train Gianluca and Pietro, an Italian check airman. We would practice our maneuvers over the Adriatic then fly to Rimini or Ancona to practice patterns and landings. It was a very pleasant two weeks indeed!

One last humorous Gianluca story occurred during his training. Being a civilian learning to fly a demanding military aircraft, and adding a demanding instructor pilot, G would sometimes complain and make excuses for his less-than-sterling performance. I would try to thicken up G's skin by saying, "G, don't be a pussy!"

A year or two later we were talking on the phone, and I was complaining about something. G did not hesitate. He said, "Richie, don't be a pussee . . ." I had to laugh, because I richly deserved it!

I ferried a total of five L-39s to Europe over a four-year period, the first and last of them solo. Believe it or not I do a great job keeping myself company during these trips. These five aircraft had excellent avionics and autopilots, so once I had everything programmed on the ground, all I had to do was engage the autopilot during the climb and monitor everything while talking on the radio.

Gianluca received the first two aircraft in June and September of 2010. During that fall I received a call from a Russian businessman named Sergey Mayzus, who lived outside of Prague. He was looking to buy an L-39 and saw an advertisement we had on our website. He called and told me he had almost made another deal with a different broker, but that fellow refused to arrange a ferry flight to Europe. I told Sergey that, since I had already ferried two L-39s to Europe that year, I did not see why I couldn't ferry a third one. Before we even had a sales agreement drawn up, Sergey wired half a million dollars to me for a show-winning aircraft we had restored as well as a spare engine.

Sergey was not a pilot himself, but he loved aviation. He already owned a brand-new Cirrus SR22 and was talking about getting a Eurocopter. The deal with me was his first step in putting together an L-39 aerobatic team to fly in air shows all over Europe.

Sergey sent his personal pilot to make the ferry flight with me. Simon Attard was an intelligent young man from Malta. Flying the L-39 was going to be an unimaginable opportunity for him. He arrived only a day or two before the ferry flight, so I put him in the back seat and planned to really conduct his training once we arrived in Europe. Simon was good company, and we had an uneventful trip across the ocean and Europe.

We flew first to Bautzen, Germany, where Bernd Rehn, the former East German Air Force senior engineer for their L-39 fleet, installed some new equipment for our L-39. On an interesting side note, I got to tour the airport and see a bunker under the control tower. It was eerie to be in that dark relic of their Cold War past. We then flew to Rimini, Italy, which acts as the port of entry for San Marino, a small mountaintop city-state where the aircraft would be registered.

A few days later we flew to Prague and landed at the Aero Vodochody Airport, where the aircraft had been built three decades before. For the next four months I would fly to Prague for about one week every month and train Simon. However, that first night in Prague was the most memorable.

Sergey had been a former Soviet naval officer, and it seemed he wanted to challenge me to a political debate that first night. I remember him saying, "Richard, Russia is an empire. Why does America think it has the right to interfere?"

My response was, "Sergey, I am a pilot, not a politician. I delivered your airplane and will train your pilot. Leave the geopolitics to the politicians." We got along just fine after that.

Sergey was an interesting guy. In his young thirties, he ran his own investment and currency-exchange service. Obviously, this made him a wealthy man. It was interesting getting to understand his mentality. Sergey lived in a thirty-thousand-square-foot chateau an hour south of Prague on sixty hectares of land. He had a small army of Ukrainian workers who took care of the property and the house. It was a bit like watching a medieval lord rule over his castle. I once asked him how he had become so wealthy. He responded, "Richard, do not worry. All my money is above the table." That made me smile.

That first night in Prague was quite memorable. Sergey told me, "Richard, we will go out tonight. We will eat. We will drink. We will go to the clubs. I will spend eight or nine thousand euros." And that is exactly what we did. Four guys spent a long night of eating, drinking, and being merry. We took a taxi home as the sun came up and we did not get any flight training accomplished the next day.

Simon was fun to train. He was a smart young man and very capable pilot. Having only a few hundred hours of flight experience, I got to train him exactly as I would a military student pilot. Later that winter we flew to Rimini, where Pietro gave Simon his L-39 check ride. Simon took off in winter fog, flew to the Italian mountainous middle where he completed his maneuvers, then flew an instrument approach to minimums back at Rimini. Pietro, who was a former Italian Air Force F-104 pilot, later told me, "Rich, you trained Simon very well."

I responded, "Did you expect anything less?"

I was in Prague one December, training Simon, and Sergey was in Kaliningrad, Russia, east of Poland. He called me and said, "Richard, it is cold here. Come get me!" So that is what I did. Our European handler got a clearance for me to fly the L-39 to Russia the next day, and I flew solo to Kaliningrad. On arrival everyone was amazed to see this military aircraft in NATO colors and civilian registration. The first person to greet me was the customs agent. He just held out his hand and said, "passport," which I had nearly left back in Prague! I flew Sergey to Prague that afternoon and then to Malta the next day, where we spent most of a week basking in the relative warmth of the Mediterranean, flying during the day, and gambling at night. Life was good!

Simon and Sergey had a falling out sometime after that, and I started training another pilot for Sergey, a young Czech fellow named Dobroslav Chrobak. Dob was also a very good pilot, and we had much fun during his training in the Czech Republic and Slovakia. He liked to fly cross country, so we flew all over that area. We were also invited to numerous airports to put on aerobatic displays. We really enjoyed ourselves.

Sergey and I stay in touch to this day, but I have not visited him for quite a few years. He eventually sold the three L-39s he bought from me. Of course, flying itself was a big reason I so enjoyed this time in my life, but I also greatly enjoyed becoming friends with and exploring the cities of like-minded people from other countries.

An additional bonus was taking Rosann to many of these interesting places for her to enjoy the travel and camaraderie. Sergey and I were in his kitchen drinking beer late one night. He suddenly said, "Richard, Anna wants to meet Rosann."

I said, "Sergey, I can't get her on a flight this week."

Sergey held up a finger as if to say *wait a moment*. He then grabbed his tablet, and after pecking away for a few minutes said, "Ha! I can get her a ticket for only three thousand dollars!" So that is what we did. Sergey rarely took no for an answer, and he was always very generous.

An interesting note—Dob and a Swiss businessman bought an L-39, N139LL, from Sergey a few years ago. It is now hangared at the Trenčín Airfield in Slovakia, home of LOTN, an aircraft overhaul factory. Each year in October, I travel to Piešťany, a spa-resort town not far from Bratislava, and we conduct two weeks of training in Lima-Lima. So, I am still enjoying the pleasures of international travel and interesting worldwide friends.

In the spring of 2013, I received a call from a fellow Delta Air Lines and warbird pilot, Paul Keppeler. Paul lives in Wisconsin and owns a former Royal Canadian Air Force CT-133 Silver Star. Basically, this is a Lockheed T-33 jet trainer that the Canadians built under license. They modified the rear fuselage and installed a British Rolls-Royce Nene engine with over a thousand pounds more thrust. One of these CT-133s had been sold to a Royal Norwegian Air Force pilot, and he wanted it ferried to Norway.

Paul and I had flown together at some air shows and on the B-777 at Delta, so we knew each other well. He asked if I could arrange for the export permission and ferry the aircraft with him. I said sure and started the very long and involved process of getting permission from the US Department of State to export a military-controlled item. This involves much more paperwork and coordination than you can possibly imagine and usually takes eight weeks. I had the permission in three weeks, which had to be a record!

Paul sent me the flight manual for the aircraft so I could study and prepare for my training and check ride. I trained with an instructor friend of Paul's and got my rating from Larry Salganek in Santa Fe, New Mexico. I showed up in Rockford, Illinois, a couple days early. Paul and I performed a test flight and declared the airplane ready for the ferry flight.

We planned an early takeoff and a long first leg to Quebec. This old airplane really sucked down the fuel, so getting a clearance to high altitude became critical for a long-range flight. I spent part of the night talking to Chicago and Toronto ATC to arrange an unrestricted climb to thirty-five thousand feet. All was set, but once we were airborne the next morning, they didn't know what we were talking about. The request had never been passed along. We were eventually assigned thirty-three thousand feet and landed uneventfully in Quebec with a thirty-minute fuel reserve. The next leg to Goose Bay was shorter, and we put the airplane to bed for the night.

The second day was also uneventful, with two shorter legs of 675 nm to Narsarsuaq, Greenland, and 650 nm to Keflavík, Iceland. The third day was going to be the challenge, a nearly thousand-nautical-mile-run direct to Stavanger, Norway. We were cleared by Iceland to thirty-five thousand feet, and I arranged direct routing that cut a hundred miles off the route. However, Paul's oxygen mask was leaking and mine was malfunctioning, trying to force-feed oxygen to me under pressure. It was a very uncomfortable leg, and we were both relieved to arrive in Norway.

The aircraft owner, Martin Tesli, call sign Tin Tin, would not arrive from the NATO-wide "Tiger Meet" exercise until the next day. I received a very pleasant surprise when a Norwegian aviation inspector showed up to fly with me for my low-altitude waiver for the air show we would be attending that weekend. It turned out to be a former colleague from my ENJJPT days, Rolf Meum. We flew that afternoon, I performed low-altitude aerobatics for Rolf, I signed him off for his checkout in the T-33, and we then flew formation with Martin in his F-16. This was going to be a very cool weekend!

Paul left to go home for his daughter's high school graduation, and I stayed to fly in the air show each day, putting the T-33 through its paces. I then flew commercial to Germany. My wife met me there and we took the high-speed train from Frankfurt to Bautzen, where Bernd Rehn promised to show us around that week. We went to museums, drove to Gorlitz, Poland, and generally enjoyed a mini vacation. Rosann then flew home, and I flew back to Norway to fly the T-bird up to Bodø, north of the Arctic Circle for another weekend air show at the RNLAF F-16 base.

Since it was June, we were in Bodø around the summer solstice. Basically, the sun does not go down at night. That Saturday night we went into town and had some fun at a local bar with the other air show performers. I kept looking out the window for it to get dark as a reminder to go back to my room for some sleep. That never happened. Finally, Martin tapped me on the shoulder, and we trudged back to our rooms for a few hours of shut-eye.

This was a great trip, and Martin and I were to repeat it again later in August. That June in Stavanger and Bodø, they were celebrating one hundred years of the RNLAF. In August we flew the T-bird to North Weald near London to celebrate seventy years since the Norwegians set up two Spitfire squadrons during WWII. I got to fly the memorials at North Weald and then the T-33 solo to Duxford for one of the coolest displays of WWII aircraft.

Martin and I then flew visually up the east coast of the UK to the RAF Leuchars air base near Edinburgh, Scotland, for another big air show. What a tremendous view flying along the entire edge of the English Channel and seeing the northern UK countryside!

Since Tin Tin and I arrived in Edinburgh early in the week, we had a few days off before the air show was to begin. We had our wives fly in commercially, and then we rented a car and drove to Loch Ness. We stayed at a bed-and-breakfast on the south side of the lake and enjoyed a few days of relaxation before returning for the Leuchars air show. No, there was no sign of Nessie, the Loch Ness monster, during our stay.

CHAPTER 26

Nigeria, Brazil, and Beyond

Over the next three or four years IJ sold three L-39s to two different customers in Brazil. The export permissions were more difficult and time-consuming for these aircraft. The word I got from our consultant in DC was that some of the South American clients who imported L-39s had not followed the US mandatory restrictions in the past. Being military fighter/trainer-type airplanes, US ITAR (International Traffic in Arms Regulations) is very strict about export permission, where they can go, and what they can be used for.

For the first aircraft to Brazil, I had a young Brazilian pilot named Rafael with me who would learn to fly the L-39 for the new owner, Valmir. Rafa was a very good pilot and a pleasure to do this long, five-thousand-nautical-mile trip with. We ferried the aircraft to south Florida the first day and then island-hopped our way to South America. The Caribbean is a beautiful place, and the islands we stayed at made us want to stay longer than just overnight. We stayed in Providenciales in Turks and Caicos and Antigua, both incredibly beautiful.

We avoided Venezuela as we worried their government might seize our aircraft on some trumped-up pretense. The next stops after crossing the Caribbean were Georgetown, Guyana, and Cayenne, French Guiana. I did not really care for these locations, but I wish I'd had more time to explore, as I found out the French penal colony of *Papillon* fame was only one hundred miles away from Cayenne.

When we left French Guiana behind and crossed five hundred miles of virgin Amazon jungle into northern Brazil, I spent an hour looking down at an unbroken triple-canopy jungle without a single road or village in sight. Engine don't fail me now!

Our first stop and layover in Brazil was Macapá, located exactly on the equator and the Amazon River. Macapá is an interesting place. The river is many kilometers across and close enough to the mouth of the Amazon to have significant tidal changes. My favorite memory of Macapá is eating at several restaurants with the most amazing fish dishes. Grilled pacu, tucunaré, or filhote in a white cream sauce topped with shrimp were to die for.

We continued our journey south through Brasília and finally arrived in Rio de Janeiro. ANAC, Brazil's civilian-aviation authority, would take a week to process our permission and entry taxes, so I flew Delta home to Atlanta and returned a week later for the last leg of the trip to a small uncontrolled airport near São Paulo. ATC tried to route me quite a distance north and then near major thunderstorms. I refused based on fuel burn and obvious safety concerns. Finally, when I descended through 14,500 feet, I canceled my instrument flight plan and proceeded visually to the Itápolis Airport, where I performed a little impromptu air show. There were dozens of people waiting, and they enthusiastically welcomed me after my arrival.

The next two aircraft for Brazil were sold to two wonderful partners, Edio and Guilherme. These fellows had been friends since their school days. Their families are close, and they live in two beautiful houses on one large tract of land. Edio's family owns huge cattle ranches in the north of Brazil, and Guilherme builds large commercial buildings such as hotels.

In fact, while in Florianópolis, I stayed on Santa Catarina Island in a hotel Guilherme owned. The island reminded me of North Island in San Diego, with a bridge connecting it to the mainland. The view of the mountains and the bay was truly remarkable, and the stores and restaurants along the shoreline made this a desirable vacation spot for people from all over southern South America.

I trained their pilot Wagner and the two owners. My Portuguese is limited, but my Spanish is pretty good. Between those two languages and English, I had a great time introducing each of these three gentlemen to the nuances of the L-39.

I need to mention that their buying agent in the US was a fellow Brazilian named Jose Barth Freitas. Barth is an experienced commercial pilot and runs an export business in Fort Lauderdale. His main home is in Tutui, north of São Paulo. I learned a lot from him about how to move an aircraft to Brazil in the most cost-effective manner.

Barth planned some different stops in the Caribbean as well as coordinated our refueling at small uncontrolled airfields in Brazil to avoid outrageously high landing fees and fuel costs. He also used a different handler, which saved us 40 percent on fuel from the first ferry.

We stopped for the night at his home airport, Tutui, before delivering that first aircraft to Florianópolis the next day. Barth was friends with everyone in his town, including the police chief, a doctor, and the mayor. They all came to his house that night for a big barbecue in his outdoor courtyard. What a great party!

The next day was one leg to São José Airport, where Edio, Guilherme, and many friends were awaiting our arrival. Again, I asked ATC for permission for high speed and maneuvers and did an impromptu air show on arrival. God, how I was loving this job!

I ferried the third and last L-39 to Brazil with Wagner the next year. The mission was uneventful until our arrival in Barbados. We arrived with the remnants of a tropical depression dumping heavy rain on the island. The fueler refused to fuel our aircraft because of the rain, so we spent the night and left the next day.

When we arrived late in the day in Macapá, it was the start of a long religious holiday weekend. We would be stuck there for four days. It was a little tedious, but Wagner and I certainly ate our fill of locally caught fish.

We finally left late one afternoon after the holiday, and we landed in the dark at one of those small uncontrolled airports. Nothing like a "black hole" approach in the middle of nowhere! We passed through Barth's airport and continued to Florianópolis the next day.

These trips across the North Atlantic Ocean and the Amazon jungle were certainly challenging, and they had their own set of risks with long legs, cold ocean water, and a forbidding tropical landscape. However, I had become quite an expert at planning and executing these missions. I believe these first nine missions were just what I needed to get prepared for what would come next, the delivery of four fighter aircraft from the US West Coast to West Africa.

I had mentioned earlier that the Nigerian Air Force purchased four Dornier Alpha Jets from two operators of the type here in the US. These were retired German Air Force aircraft that had been exported to the US. About half of the two dozen aircraft ended up in Canada being used for military-contract flying. The other half were sold mostly to US military-contract companies with a handful going to private owners.

The Nigerians originally bought two dozen French-built Alpha Jets but lost several of theirs to crashes over the years. The basic systems are nearly identical between the Dassault and Dornier versions, with the major difference being a tactical navigation system and uprated engines in the German version. Two of the four aircraft needed in-depth maintenance, and the fourth one had not yet been assembled, since it had been imported from Germany.

The sellers promised to provide ferry pilots at first but reneged on that promise after the sale. The Nigerian embassy finally called me, as they were told no one in the US had my level of experience ferrying these types of aircraft to overseas destinations.

We negotiated a contract for me to deliver the four aircraft to Nigeria. Unfortunately, the aircraft were in bad shape—plus the last one was yet to be assembled and flight tested—so I ended up delivering one each year for four years in a row. These would prove to be the most challenging missions I had faced to date.

I ferried the first aircraft in March 2014, solo with no autopilot. That meant I would hand-fly with sensitive controls for four or five days and seven thousand nautical miles across three continents. I can honestly say that, even on the first leg to Edmonton, Canada, I was only just beginning to realize what a challenge I had accepted.

March is springtime, right? Not in Canada it wasn't! My second leg was from Edmonton to Churchill on the southwest coast of Hudson Bay. Churchill is known for its polar bear population, and it was -20 degrees Celsius on arrival. I fueled, confirmed the next flight plan, and took off for a 650-nautical-mile run all the way across a mostly frozen Hudson Bay for Frobisher Bay on Baffin Island, otherwise known as Nunavut. It was a chilly -25 degrees in Frobisher Bay. I had to take the nickel-cadmium (NiCad) battery out of the aircraft and store it indoors so it would not freeze overnight!

The morning preparations were brutal. At -25 with a blowing wind, you could not stay outside for more than ten minutes before needing to go inside and thaw out. The aircraft had frost on the wings. I called for a deicing truck, but in the thirty minutes it took for that truck to arrive, the wind sublimated the frost off the aircraft. That means it went from a solid to a gas without first becoming water. Amazing!

On my first attempt to start the engines, they almost exceeded the exhaust gas temperature (EGT) limits. I asked for forced-air heat blankets to be applied to each engine, and they finally started normally. However, the cold shrunk the seals on my canopy and nosewheel strut so that the nitrogen charge leaked out. I would not be able to service either one again until my arrival in Nigeria three days later. I can tell you that canopy is heavy to operate without the cushion of the nitrogen charge. I also made darn sure to taxi and land smoothly until the nosewheel strut could be serviced.

As I flew across the Davis Strait to Sondrestrom, Greenland, I was very happy to have two engines versus only one in the L-39 and T-33. The next two days went quite smoothly as I hopped, skipped, and jumped across Greenland, Iceland, England, France, and Spain to Palma de Mallorca in the Mediterranean. However, the last day across North and West Africa would offer everything in its power to fail the mission.

I left Palma the next morning and set my course to Tamanrasset in southern Algeria, land of the Tuareg people, not Volkswagens. I was facing one thousand nautical miles of Sahara Desert and a stiff quartering headwind. I asked ATC for thirty-five thousand feet, and they cleared me to climb. The aircraft did not have all the internationally required equipment to be at that altitude, but I knew I could get my total fuel flow down to four hundred kilos per hour. With two thousand kilos of fuel on board, I would be able to land with a solid hour reserve. ATC then asked me, "Nigerian Air Force 477, are you RVSM equipped?"

My response was quick and assured. "No, sir, but I can hold my altitude really well."

They thought about that for ten seconds then quipped, "Okay."

Tamanrasset is a joint civilian/military airport in the middle of the desert. Mine was the only aircraft I saw operating that day. I cleared customs, filed my final flight plan to Abuja, Nigeria, and asked about the promised ground power unit (GPU). I was told it was broken. Here I was at a hot, high-elevation airport. To start the first engine on the battery required a minimum of twenty-five volts from a twenty-four-volt battery! I had the minimum, and thankfully the left engine started normally. I pushed the power up on the left engine and used its twenty-eight-volt generator to get the second engine started.

I was a bit concerned about the last leg. It would be 850 nautical miles into a roaring 150-knot wind from the west at altitude. The aircraft had eighty-two-gallon external fuel tanks without which I would not have been able to plan and fly the mission. What do you know, Murphy's Law was hard at work. Shortly after leveling off at cruise altitude, I realized the right drop tank wasn't feeding. As I crossed Niger into Nigeria, I considered stopping at Kano or Kaduna for fuel. However, I calculated I could land at Abuja with a thirty-minute reserve. I tried to declare minimum fuel, but the radios were extremely busy, and Nigerian ATC just did not seem to understand my situation.

As I passed over Kaduna, ATC wanted me to start an early descent. I refused the clearance and reiterated my marginal fuel state. Then they tried to get me to fly out to a navigational fix in preparation for a full instrument procedure. I did not have another ten to fifteen minutes worth of fuel to waste, so I refused again. I told them I would proceed directly to the airport for a visual approach.

Abuja is the capital city, but the airport only has one runway, and both ground control and tower operate on the same frequency. To say the radio was busy is an understatement. As I leveled off abeam the runway, the tower cleared an airliner into position and hold on the runway. I was livid. I keyed the microphone, and in a very commanding voice blurted, "Get that aircraft off the runway now!" The airliner's captain understood what was happening and turned off at the next taxiway. I landed safely with the low-fuel lights just starting to blink as I taxied to the military ramp.

After I shut down the engines, one of my engineering friends held up a cell phone and said, "Rich, the tower wants to talk to you."

I angrily retorted, "Well, I don't want to talk to them. Tell them to listen up the next time someone declares a fuel emergency!" That was the end of it. We were met by many of the NAF headquarters staff, including a two-star general who told me how much he appreciated what I had accomplished . . . solo.

The next year I ferried the second Alpha Jet with an NAF fighter pilot in the rear seat. I had trained Henry, and headquarters wanted him to have the experience of this challenging and demanding mission. At the end of day one, I had to shoot a full instrument approach into Frobisher Bay to ILS minimums. I don't know if Henry was more scared or impressed by the situation as he watched me descend toward mountain peaks poking up through the low clouds. It certainly drove home for him the need for aggressively precise execution in the face of less-than-ideal weather.

Henry could not make the third ferry the following year, so I took John Stewart with me. John is ten years older than me and a retired USAF fighter pilot who flew everything from the F-100 in Vietnam to the F-16 afterward. He also teaches in the Alpha Jet, so he was the perfect ferry partner.

As we worked our way across Canada, it became evident that our encoding transponder was malfunctioning. You can still be cleared to fly without it in North America, but by the time we got to Iceland on the second day, we were informed we would not be allowed in European airspace without it. I had an avionics technician come out and test the old military unit. He said it was weak but serviceable.

On day three I landed at Manchester, England, changed out of our survival gear, and filed for Palma de Mallorca. As Scottish control was about to hand us over to London, we were informed our transponder had again failed and we would not be allowed to continue. Darn! So we flew back to Manchester. I tried to get someone, anyone, with a transponder test box to come out and check our equipment, but no one was willing to help. Very frustrating indeed!

The next day I did a short flight around the radar pattern and Manchester reported our unit was working again. We fueled up, filed another flight plan, and were on our way. Would you believe it, as London was about to hand us off to the French controller, the transponder failed again! We ended up landing at Farnborough outside of London. An avionics technician again came out to test our transponder, and I was informed it was weak but operational.

I began to suspect the unit was affected by the temperature and pressure changes at altitude. So, late in the afternoon, I filed a low-altitude flight across France and Spain with only just enough altitude to clear the Pyrenees Mountains. That did the trick. The transponder worked the whole way to Palma.

The next morning, we took off for Tamanrasset. Shortly after crossing the Algerian coast, Algerian control asked us to cycle our transponder. It had finally failed completely. However, it no longer mattered. The rest of the route would be in a nonradar environment. Problem solved!

The last Alpha Jet ferry was supposed to happen in August 2018. This was the aircraft that had not been assembled since it left Germany a decade before. Mike Lee and I have worked together on Nigerian Air Force Alpha Jets for fourteen years. NAF contracted him to prepare each of these aircraft for their ferry delivery. Mike always did a great job, but it took him until the first week of December to get this final aircraft ready to go. The test flights out of Arlington, Washington, went flawlessly, and we prepared for the final mission.

The first two days of the ferry mission were brutal. I had another NAF fighter pilot with me, so I appreciated the backup. However, every stop in Canada, Greenland, and Iceland was a howling winter wonderland. Edmonton, Churchill, Frobisher Bay, Sondrestrom, and Reykjavík were setting snowfall records. Thankfully the Alpha Jet is a very robust aircraft. At each station I would borrow a broom and sweep the cold, dry snow off the aircraft's wings, tail, and fuselage, then quickly start up and get out of Dodge before it accumulated again.

With the short winter days, we arrived at Reykjavík, Iceland, at night. I had landed there three times before, rather than at the joint-use airport in Keflavík just twelve miles away, because Reykjavík was the only place enroute where I could get liquid oxygen (LOX) to fill the crew's ten-liter oxygen tank. About the time I was turning onto the ILS final approach, approach control told us the airport manager said he would not allow us to land because we were a military flight. He said I would have to divert to Keflavík. There was nothing I could do except comply as I did not want to waste my reserve-fuel holding while arguing our case.

Keflavík is a great airport with ten-thousand-foot-long runways and full services. I landed there, put the aircraft to bed, and went to a hotel for the night. We awoke to a winter storm that blew in overnight. Thankfully we had fueled the night before. File a flight plan, broom the snow off the aircraft, and slip-slide our way to the active runway. Sitting at the end of the runway, I was watching the snow start to accumulate again on my wings. I warned the tower we needed a quick takeoff clearance or else we would have to go back to the ramp to refuel and clean off the aircraft. We were finally cleared, and as I climbed out of that winter landscape, I breathed a sigh of relief.

England was balmy with clear skies and temperatures in the fifties. Ah ha, but Ole Murphy wasn't done with us yet. I was informed that because we did not give Algeria two weeks' notice (we gave them ten days' notice), they would not approve our diplomatic clearance to overfly and land in Tamanrasset. It took me a few hours to figure out an alternative plan. So, we filed for Madrid instead of Palma and planned to fly an end run around Algeria the next day with fuel stops in Morocco and Mali.

As we were letting down into Madrid, ATC again questioned letting us land at the international airport versus Torrejón Air Base a short distance to the east. The big issue would have been contracting a large fuel truck to travel by road to the air base to fuel us, a very, very expensive proposition. Madrid finally relented and allowed us to land as planned.

The end run would cost me an extra thousand nautical miles and a few thousand dollars in fuel. Ouch! But there really was no other good option. The next day, the end run to Al Massira in Morocco was fast and easy. We then took off, flew south around the southwest corner of Algeria, and headed to Gao, Mali, another thousand-nautical-mile run. The service people treated us just fine at Gao, but it was plain to see this was a very basic third-world facility. Of even more interest was the huge French military compound that made up the east side of the airport.

Just as we were about to start engines for our last leg into Abuja, two French military officers arrived beside our aircraft. It seemed the French joint forces commander (JFAC) wanted to know what an active-duty fighter was doing there, and whether we would interfere with his operation. We convinced them of our intent to leave and fly away, but we were held in the cockpit for a couple of hours before we were finally cleared to depart. Then the controller had a difficult time getting our departure clearance. We were extremely happy and relieved to finally leave Gao.

If nothing else, all these international ferry missions certainly established my credentials as an experienced pilot who could consistently get a challenging mission accomplished even under difficult circumstances. But more than that, I had said a prayer when I retired from the air force years before that I wanted to find a job that used all my skills and experience. I had certainly found a niche no one else could claim.

I was honored when Dale "Snort" Snodgrass from Draken International called one day to ask about ferrying aircraft across the Atlantic. Seemed Draken had purchased a fleet of A-4s that were in Germany and needed to be brought back to the US. I would not be part of the mission itself, but I very much appreciated Dale picking my brain about planning it.

Unrelated to the ferry missions, I've had the chance to work with some other professional pilot groups in this warbird community. I helped train the Cirrus Jet and Learjet Bombardier test pilots in the L-39 when they were using it for chase duty and envelope exploration. I also validated the Honda Jet test pilots as they prepared to do formation demonstrations at major air shows.

Over a seventeen-year period, I have managed to accumulate over four thousand hours flying military aircraft from ten foreign countries, with the hours equally split between piston and turbine aircraft. Add my eight thousand USAF hours, and almost half of my twenty-eight thousand flight hours are in military fighter, trainer, and transport aircraft.

After several US airplane crashes, the FAA mandated that airline pilots practice their proficiency in the simulator without the aid of flight directors, autopilots, or autothrottles. I found those maneuvers easy to do because flying these warbirds keeps your hand skills and hand-eye coordination sharp. I wish every professional pilot would have such opportunities.

I have trained folks in warbirds, aerobatics, and formation. Some come from pilot backgrounds where such maneuvers were never required. These pilots come from every walk of life, and I tell every one of them that their skills will be better for the training. Some tend to blow me off initially, but eventually they all admit the truth of my words. Helping other pilots fly safer is one of the most rewarding accomplishments of my flying career. I would not have given up those opportunities for anything.

CHAPTER 27

Retirement

I titled this chapter "Retirement," but as you will come to see, it's a bit of a misnomer. I retired from the United States Air Force in September 2002 after thirteen years on active duty and fifteen years in the Air National Guard. Performing my Air National Guard duty concurrently with my airline job, I flew for Delta Air Lines for thirty-one and a half years, retiring in November 2018.

The FAA strictly regulates all facets of aviation in the US and dictates that Part 121 pilots (flying for the airlines) must retire at age sixty-five regardless of physical or mental condition. I admit I especially enjoyed my last eleven years flying the Boeing 777, even if being on an airplane for up to eighteen hours was a physically and mentally exhausting activity. I don't want to sound greedy, but the airline job was actually a great way to make a living, and the pay had recovered quite nicely a dozen years after Delta exited bankruptcy. That more-than-adequate salary would certainly be missed.

The funny part about the FAA's arbitrary rulemaking is that you can fly business jets at any age so long as you can pass a Class II medical, which is less demanding than the Class I required for airline and any international flying. So, there you are in the same airspace, at the same altitudes, as all those airliners. Of course, in this case you might only be carrying a dozen clients versus two hundred or even three hundred passengers.

The pay is good, but it is not like working for Delta, American, or United. What most people do not realize is how much harder a business jet pilot must work compared to his or her fellow airline compadres. In the airlines, you are handed a computerized flight plan, weather forecast, and list of Notices to Airmen (NOTAMs). You brief the flight attendant crew, preflight the aircraft, and go fly. You have a dispatcher to conduct all the flight planning and arrange for all required permissions, notifications, etc. A fueler refuels the aircraft. A cabin team cleans the aircraft after each leg. The catering crew brings all the food and beverages on board before pushback. Baggage handlers load the aircraft. A hotel and layover team arranges for crew transportation and a hotel. All you need to do is fly the airplane from point A to point B. Easy, right?

It is very different for the typical business jet pilot. You do your own flight and fuel planning. You clean the aircraft. You arrange for catering, fueling, hotels, and transportation. You load the bags! To leave or enter the US involves some very specific and complex rules and procedures. You handle all of that, and you do it sometimes for some rather unpleasant clients. Thankfully most of them are very nice and thoughtful people, but not all of them.

The airlines count being on time (plus or minus fifteen minutes) for departure and arrival as a vital statistic and an important marketing tool. In private jet flying, I have seen a client show up two or three hours late with no communication to the crew. Also, when an airline says its flight number X is flying from point A to point B, that is what it does unless there is a significant reason to do otherwise—weather, mechanical failure, or passenger emergency. Not so in the business jet world.

The German general Helmuth von Moltke once said no plan survives first contact with the enemy. The clients usually are not your enemy, but darn if the initial plan to fly them from point A to point B ends up looking like A to C, then B, and maybe onward to D afterward. And, oh, can you order us a car at C and last-minute meals at B? You get the picture. And you do all this for a fraction of the pay your airline brothers and sisters are earning. It can be very frustrating after forty years of performing as part of an operation that values precision planning and execution.

I say all this because when I retired from Delta in November 2018, I did not yet feel ready to just kick back, go fishing, and play with the grandkids. My first real exposure to business jets came in 2017. My best friend BJ Kennamore called me. It seemed a local company in Muscle Shoals, Alabama, had a brand-new Embraer Phenom 100 jet and no one to fly it. They had lost their regular pilot to the regional airlines and the jet was just sitting in the hangar gathering dust.

The Phenom 100 is a nice jet aircraft. You can seat eight people, including the pilots, carry plenty of bags, and with a light payload travel about one thousand nautical miles. It has a nicely integrated cockpit with modern glass panel displays.

I interviewed and was hired on a part-time basis. I went through the month-long training at CAE in Dallas and started flying the family around for business and pleasure trips all around the South, but mostly down to their condo in Destin, in the Florida panhandle. I figured this would be a good arrangement to keep me adequately busy after retirement from Delta in a year. Of course, no good thing lasts. The family decided to sell the airplane after the elderly patriarch of the family became ill.

I have another friend in the Atlanta area named Bob Brown. He and a businessman friend, Ron Sewell, bought an L-39 jet warbird some years before, and I trained each of them. Ron owned a Citation 650 at the time, an older but very capable business jet. Bob checked me out in the right seat, and I flew second in command (SIC) on a few trips.

As I was getting close to retiring from Delta in mid-2018, I started talking to Bob about the chance to come fly for him. He manages the maintenance and crewing for about a dozen business jet owners. His managed fleet changes from time to time but has included Citations, French Falcons, Gulfstreams, and Challengers. These names might mean little to anyone outside of aviation, but they run the gamut of size, speed, range, and payload.

Bob started by getting me SIC rated in the Citations and Falcons. I have spent most of my time in the Falcon 50 and 900, three-engine, international-range aircraft. I really like the Falcon 900 and the Falcon 50 as they are treated as a single rating by the FAA. They can carry a good load off a short runway, go as fast as an airliner, fly high, and travel as far as four thousand nautical miles.

The clients are usually men, but not always. They are typically in their mid-years and own a very successful business that justifies a private jet for important meetings as well as family vacations. I have carried professional football and basketball stars, captains of industry, political powerhouses, and A-list celebrities.

As I said, most of these people carry themselves well and show the crew respect and appreciation. But sometimes they leave the airplane cabin in such a sorry state you would have thought a troop of monkeys had used it for their playground!

Part of the pleasure of private flying is sometimes bringing Rosann along. Most clients are accommodating, and I have taken Rosann to Monterrey, California, and various Caribbean destinations. I am sure there will be many more fun destinations for us in the foreseeable future.

I must give Bob a lot of credit. Running any business is a constantly challenging proposition, but aviation seems to be even more so. The expenses are sky high with high-dollar aircraft and expensive aircrew, maintenance, insurance, and hangar costs. Couple the large capital and overhead expenses with owners or clients who drag out paying their bills to the last possible moment, and you can imagine the frustration of constantly juggling cash flow to stay afloat. When I ran International Jets, the one activity I hated with every cell in my body was figuratively getting on my knees and begging clients to pay us what they owed.

For a couple of months, flying for Bob slowed down to the point that I started looking for other flying jobs. I had applied to several companies, but I'm sure being sixty-five years old is a perceived negative to many employers due to international rules about pilot age. Too bad, because I am healthy, willing to work hard, and bring a depth of experience that cannot be matched.

I advertised on one Facebook page and got an immediate response from Trident Aircraft, a charter outfit in Maryland. I only flew for Trident for a few months, but I really liked them. Nicole, the scheduler, was always accommodating and treated me very well. I started flying the Phenom 100 that they managed. The Canadian owner was married to an American and they lived on the East Coast.

I am qualified to fly the Phenom single pilot, but Trident's insurance insisted there always be a copilot on board. So, Steven Kovarik and I became tied at the hip for these trips. Steven is a great guy. He's young with hopes of becoming a future senior corporate or airline pilot. As a very experienced instructor, I worked with Steven until Trident finally put him through Pilot-in-Command (PIC) school. Now that Steven was rated in the Phenom, I had basically promoted myself out of a job. Hmm, what to do next?

One of my good friends is Bob Lutz, the retired vice chairman of General Motors. Bob was a marine corps fighter pilot, and along with owning jet warbirds, he also owned a Citation 650. Since I already had my SIC rating in that aircraft, Bob asked if I could get my PIC rating, since I was retired from the airlines. He was having trouble finding a pilot crew to fly him and his wife Terri on business trips and to his vacation home on Montserrat in the Caribbean. Sunshine and sandy beaches? Sign me up!

I got my PIC rating and flew a couple of trips on Bob's aircraft. My copilot was usually Brian Senor, a nice Christian fellow from Saginaw, Michigan. I have acted as Bob's instructor pilot for years, flying out of Willow Run Airport just west of Detroit Metro Airport. Willow Run's claim to fame is the B-24 Liberator bomber factory that the Ford Motor

Company operated during World War II. Ford built nearly seven thousand bombers, as well as kits for almost two thousand more.

A side note about Bob: He truly was a captain of the automotive industry. With over fifty years of experience, even to this day in his nineties he is widely known as the "Car Guy." He is also the de facto leader of an email group we affectionately named the "Lutz Gang." I pale in comparison with some of its members, other captains of industries that hail from around the world. However, I am extremely honored to be a part of this sage group.

Shortly after I got my PIC rating in Bob's Citation, he informed me he would be trading in his jet to NetJets, a fractional-ownership company. They would be giving him access to a brand-new Citation Latitude. I cannot blame him as the new airplane was beautiful, exceptionally well equipped, and his access would cost about the same as outright ownership without any of the headaches of insurance, hangar, or maintenance. Gosh, every time I find a good gig it seems to go away! Oh well. I was sure there would be something next.

For the summer of 2019, it seemed next up would be a lot of L-39 flying. Several new owners needed training for their rating, and I ended up with three students. One of them was a fellow in Manassas, Virginia. Phil was an interesting businessman who had developed lasers that can be used by aircraft to measure airspeed, angle of attack, and position. In fact, a version of his system was used in the F-117 stealth fighter.

Another student was my Canadian friend Jeremy. Jeremy provides industrial pump and power systems for oil-field work in Canada and many other applications throughout the Pacific. Jeremy finally received his rating in June 2019, and we were all very happy for him.

The third student I started working with was a former USAF B-52 bomber pilot. He was born and raised in Atlanta and trained as an engineer at Georgia Tech. Tim is six foot three and a black belt in a Japanese martial art form. I am always in awe of the warbird-aviation community's variety of talent and interests.

Bob Brown started to use me again in the summer of 2019. I didn't mind flying the Citation 650 for his client in Salt Lake City, but I really liked flying the Falcon 900 from the PDK airport in Atlanta. I flew often with Jamie Chappell, a fellow "damn Yankee" who has made his home in the Atlanta area. You know what a damn Yankee is, right? We came to the South, liked it, and never went back North!

Jamie and I were like Batman and Robin. Since he was the PIC, I guess that made me Robin. We flew all over the country and to the Caribbean. We suffered some long days, sometimes fifteen hours or more. We even had a main hydraulic-system failure that we handled very well. I landed back at PDK with no flaps, spoilers, steering, or reverser. We did the emergency procedure by the book, and it all worked out fine. It's just incredibly nice to fly with a fellow professional who is extremely competent, someone you can trust in any situation.

At the time, Bob Brown was making an offer for a second Falcon 900. I was looking forward to getting my PIC rating when that happened and flying these aircraft all over North America. We even talked about some trips to Europe at the end of the summer. Now that would truly be a pleasure, crossing the cold North Atlantic Ocean in the comfort of a beautiful, three-engine business jet as opposed to the cockpit of an old single-engine fighter aircraft!

I think the takeaway from this part of my life had more than one element. First, I didn't feel ready to retire. I'm healthy, motivated, and still wanted to use my extensive aviation background to enjoy flying and maybe get a chance to impart some of my knowledge to other pilots, whether they be older warbird operators or younger pilots just trying to make their way to a good-paying career. Either way, keeping them safe is a worthy goal that still motivates me.

The second lesson I learned is that there are many very capable pilots in the corporate and business jet world who either did not make it into the airlines or chose not to pursue that career path. There are many reasons for not reaching the "big leagues." Some pilots do not have a college education, which most airlines require. Some do not want to move or commute to another city for work. Some might not have the jet hours or even enough hours to be considered competitive at the airlines.

The third lesson was realizing just how different and difficult the corporate and private jet world can be. Good jobs usually come by word of mouth or by recommendation. It can be a bit like an exclusive club, and the pay can be very low in comparison to the airlines. As a senior international, wide-body captain, I made a very nice six-figure salary and typically only worked ten to twelve days a month. But corporate and private jet pilots typically make half that much and can work twice as many days each month.

In the airlines, you work a specific number of days on reserve when you are on call. A private jet owner sometimes treats his pilots as if they are on call 24-7. You have no life and of course the owners always want to fly on weekends and holidays. I think the takeaway is that in the FAR Part 91 world (private flying), there really are no rules about duty day and minimum rest period. It is up to the individual pilot to negotiate his own terms with the owner, so he is not abused to the point of exhaustion. It can be a challenge.

The last thing I see is how an owner or client can be pushy about getting to his destination with little regard for operational considerations. Safety can be quickly compromised when an owner wants his pilots to disregard dangerous weather like low ceilings and visibility, thunderstorms, and winter weather, or when he pushes to operate a heavy, fast aircraft from marginal airports with short runways and limited availability of instrument approaches. It is very important that the captain build trust with the owner, so that he will accept his judgment about what constitutes a safe operation. Accomplishing that takes patience and maturity on the part of the PIC.

About three years ago, I flew a lot with a good friend, Lance Vickers. Lance is from the Carolinas and did a variety of things, including running a sawmill, before deciding to get back into flying as a full-time pursuit. Lance met the chief pilot for an owner group at Cobb County International Airport, just thirty minutes from my house.

Lance and I made an appointment and interviewed with Jason Helmka. Jason was chief pilot of an owner group named the Aviation Development Group (ADG). It is made up of about a dozen owners and half a dozen aircraft, plus some which are just managed and leased when needed by the owner group. They started using us on a contract basis. Then they hired Lance full-time until he got an offer from a company at the PDK airport that he could not refuse. So, they hired me full-time, and except for some warbird flying, I worked for ADG exclusively. I have flown Citations, Learjets, Gulfstreams, and Falcons for them.

I really liked this group. All the owners are nice people—they respect us and are usually on time! But of greater importance, I was treated well. I was given time off for family when needed, and I was paid right away when I submitted an invoice. You cannot imagine how frustrating it used to be begging a client to pay you for a service you supplied weeks or even months previously. Unfortunately, all good things come to an end. When ADG renewed their insurance, the underwriter refused to cover me once I turned seventy. Oh well. After only a week I was working on some other opportunities.

I still do overseas consulting for some foreign air forces. I thought that was winding down until some sizable contracts started heading my way in 2023 and 2024. I do enjoy the challenges of flying business jets, but I also love the feeling that helping train future fighter pilots brings. Maybe even a few have survived because of the lessons I taught them. It's important in a world where the likes of Boko Haram film the gruesome murders of their captured pilots.

I feel as if I have much to contribute, and I would like to do this for a few more years, or until it is no longer fun. That is something a wise old colonel once told me. He said when a job is no longer fun, I would know it and recognize that it's time to move on. He also said I should strive to do two things every day: learn something new and have a good time. I am still learning new things, whether it be a particular flight operation or a new aircraft's systems. I also love meeting new people and flying with more of these quiet, unassuming heroes who move captains of industry all over the world so they can keep the wheels of economy turning. I am, even still, after forty-eight years of flying, excited and proud to do my part in this niche of aviation.

CHAPTER 28

Nonna and Papé

At the time of writing this, I am seventy-one years old, Rosann is sixty-eight, and we've been married for fifty years. Quite an accomplishment, right? Well, we are both a bit old-fashioned and could not wait for our children to have children of their own.

Rick, our oldest, lives with Angela and her three children. She is a great gal, works hard, and seems to love Rick the way we think he deserves. Noah, their first born, is nineteen and in his second year of college. He is a good kid: quiet and helpful. Lucas is thirteen and tends to keep to himself but is coming out of his shell as he matures. Zoe is seven and can be a handful. We believe she sometimes acts out when she is not getting enough attention. It is a challenge for sure, but I must give Rick and Angela credit for dealing with all the issues of raising children.

It has been hard to stay close since they live in San Diego, so far away from Atlanta. However, Rosann and I visit them in California, and they come east for some holidays and family vacations. I think all the kids are getting comfortable with us, and I find it fascinating to see their true personalities revealed over time.

I would be remiss if I did not praise Rick. He is an apple that didn't fall far from the tree. He has the Italian good looks of his mom and the sensitive, heart-on-his-sleeve nature of his father. Rick teaches architecture and interior design at a private college in San Diego, and it is no exaggeration that his students love him. He cares so much for his students, demanding excellence in the classroom while pushing them to achieve. His record of student placement after graduation is the best his school has ever seen. I am very proud of Rick's professional accomplishments.

Angela is typical of Latina women: petite and pretty. But don't be fooled. She has impressed me as a very serious woman. She is currently working on an advanced degree in law enforcement and just passed a test for entry into the sheriff's department. We are saying prayers for her. In the meantime, she is a very dedicated life partner.

Rick suffered some serious health issues a couple of years ago that landed him in the hospital and then out of work for a few months. Angela bears a critically important responsibility for her children. No one could have faulted her if she walked away from Rick. But she did not do that. She stayed with our son and has helped him stay healthy. I cannot say enough how eternally grateful I am to her for having the maturity to commit to Rick and build a new family for the five of them.

Christina is our middle child. Typical of the stereotype, she was always quiet with a bit of a brooding persona. I remember her at the age of three or four, sneaking off to a bedroom with a pair of scissors and standing in front of a mirror while she chopped off her long hair. Rosann had worked very hard to see that Chrissy's hair grew long and straight. I literally had to hold Rosann back when she saw what a mess Chrissy had made of her hair. A willful child, Chrissy was a challenge at a very young age.

For all the stubbornness Chrissy showed us, she turned into a remarkable adult. She seems to have inherited the best physical characteristics of both Rosann and me. She has Rosann's dark Italian looks, and my physique. I remember watching her run hurdles in high school. Her fluid stride was like watching a gazelle in motion.

Chrissy attended a local university on the Hope Scholarship and lived at home. She basically cost us nothing. A few years after graduation she married her high school sweetheart and long-term boyfriend, Ryan.

Ryan is a very smart young man. He attended Georgia Tech,

one of the nation's best technical universities, earning his degree in computer engineering. In the beginning I was worried about Ryan. When school got to be too much, he would join his college buddies in nearby Buckhead on weekend nights.

Atlanta is a fun city, but like any large metropolis, you must always stay aware of your surroundings. Ryan was carjacked late one Saturday night by two men with a gun. They forced him into the passenger seat of his Mustang while one fellow drove and the other held the gun on Ryan from the back seat.

Ryan thought fast as the two threatened to kill him and told them his dad was rich and would give them money. He dialed his father and handed them the phone. Then, as the car slowed at an intersection, Ryan opened the door and rolled out onto the pavement as the two perpetrators drove away. This certainly made for an exciting story, but Ryan kept going back into Buckhead late on weekend nights. I was worried he would not survive to see graduation.

Chrissy and Ryan married in May 2008. The reception was in a house formerly owned by one of the Atlanta Coca-Cola family members. We took over the downtown Hilton and had a grand weekend.

Rosann invited many of her New York relatives to the wedding. They include some truly colorful characters. One of her cousins, Anthony, grew up on the rough-and-tumble streets of Brooklyn. Anthony basically ran a street gang while his older brother Frankie rose up through the police ranks and became a lawyer. The not-so-secret rumor was that Frankie would send some of his boys down to visit his kid brother on a regular basis to keep him on the straight and narrow. At Chrissy's wedding, Anthony pulled Rosann aside and told her, "Thanks for inviting me to the wedding. Most of the family would not have."

I remember another time in New York when we were there to celebrate Rosann's mom's birthday. Rosann's nephew Arthur was teasing our youngest daughter, Diana. Anthony got up, snuck up on Arthur, and held a knife to his crotch, telling him, "We don't treat our women that way."

Arthur blurted in surprise, "Anthony, it's me, your cousin Arthur. Don't you recognize me?" Arthur is now a seasoned Suffolk County detective on Long Island. He is not someone I would want to mess with. However, I shake my head and smile when I think about the shenanigans Anthony pulled.

Chrissy and Ryan have been divorced for over three years now. In any relationship you cannot blame just one side or the other for what went wrong. Ryan's parents went through a difficult divorce when he and his sisters were just young teens, and he never seemed to get past that.

They tried to work things out, but it seemed the die was cast. The last three years have been troublesome, trying to give their two beautiful children some sense of normalcy as they alternate households every other week. All we want is for Locklyn and Brandt to have a normal upbringing. I pray for them every day.

Chrissy has learned to stand up for herself, especially when it comes to protecting her children. That makes me very proud, and meanwhile, she has finally met a wonderful young man who we pray will be the partner she deserves. In fact, they just got engaged a few weeks ago. Rosann and I are quietly watching from the sidelines as Chrissy and RB develop their relationship.

Diana Rose is our youngest child. We knew she was special when we brought her home a few days after her birth and she smiled and laughed as we fed or changed her diaper. I used to tell Diana she is an old soul. She would watch Nick at Nite on TV. They played reruns of shows we used to watch when we were kids. Shows like *I Dream of Genie*, *The Brady Bunch*, and others kept her constant attention.

Then she fell in puppy love with musical groups like the Backstreet Boys and NSYNC. When the posters in her bedroom covered most of the walls, I told her to take them down. They quickly disappeared until I opened her closet door one day. It was like a teenybopper shrine. Girls!

Diana dated a baseball player in high school named Matt. Matt was a very nice boy: handsome, clean-cut, and respectful. Normal in every way. We really liked him. As Diana was graduating high school, she knew she was going to college at Valdosta in southern Georgia and Matt would be at a small school in the North Georgia Mountains. So, she broke up with him before leaving for Valdosta. As I look back, it was the right thing to do, but honestly, Rosann and I cried over losing Matt. We were learning a hard lesson: You cannot live your children's lives for them. They leave the nest and start making decisions for themselves, good or bad.

Diana left Valdosta and gave up a full scholarship to go to college in Colorado, where a boy she had met at Valdosta was going. He had transferred schools for his major. In six months, she dropped him too, just as he was about to propose to her. Gosh, our baby was becoming quite a heartbreaker.

Diana finished her bachelor's degree in Colorado. While still in school, she started dating another boy whom she met while serving tables. He worked as a bartender at the same restaurant. We went out to Colorado to visit her and took them to dinner. While talking to Brandon, I saw a flash in his mouth. It was a tongue piercing!

I asked him, "What's that in your mouth?"

He responded, "What?"

I retorted, "You heard me."

Rosann took one look at Brandon, then at Diana, and slapped her upside the head! I remember her doing the same thing to Rick when she found his cigarettes hidden in his dresser one morning. When he came home from school, I told him what Mom had found and that when she came home from work, she would probably yell and maybe even slap him.

I warned Rick, "You will stand there and take it!"

That is exactly what happened. Rosann walked in the door, scolded Rick, then slapped him a couple of times. A few years later at a dinner party I was telling this story and Rosann said, "I always wondered why he just stood there and took it." Rosann worked for a pulmonary doctor and saw the ravages a lifetime of smoking had on her patients. I cannot say that I blame her. Just don't let her loving, motherly demeanor fool you!

Diana graduated college and moved back home. She started dating Daniel, a future medical student. I liked Daniel. He was always a diplomat and told you what he thought you wanted to hear. But when he was at our house, Ryan would always try to rile him, verbally challenging Daniel on all subjects.

When Daniel moved to Savannah to attend medical school, Diana went with him and completed a master's degree in education. What surprised us is that she told Daniel he had one year to put a ring on her finger or else she would walk away from the relationship. And that is exactly what she did. One year later she left him after he failed to follow through. We thought she was being too tough on Daniel, with him only just completing his first year of medical school. But again, when I look back, she did the right thing.

Diana worked a few years at a privately funded school for refugee children. It seemed like a very worthwhile and rewarding endeavor. Then she suddenly got the notion that she wanted to go overseas, preferably to someplace in the third world. My aviation business helped me develop friendships and contacts all over the world. I once offered to help her find a school or charitable activity in someplace like Russia or elsewhere in Eastern Europe. Her response startled me. "But Dad, that means I'd have a bed and running water!" Lord, what kind of child had we raised?

Diana ended up spending a year teaching at a private school in China (where she certainly had a bed and running water). It was a very broadening experience, but it also showed her how a developing nation can be the land of haves and have nots. The school offered her a year extension on her contract, but she had had enough. She came back home to Atlanta and settled down to find another job.

In the meantime, Diana joined some dating websites and eventually met Mike Miller and his brother Matt. The boys are fraternal twins and a very handy duo to have around. They have been

"Hotshot" forest firefighters, and they have successfully experimented with organic farming. They are simply the kind of "can do" guys who are not afraid to tackle any project.

Mike and Diana started dating, and they seemed to be made for each other. They married and moved to Chattanooga, Tennessee. They now have two children, Josie and Charlie, four and three years old. She had some difficulty getting and staying pregnant, so we were very excited for her and Mike when they had two healthy, intelligent, rambunctious girls!

It's amazing what Mike and Diana have been doing lately. They renovated a house and opened it as an Airbnb. It's been a nonstop success. Then they bought two homes, renovated them, and recently sold both for a handsome profit. Now they've bought an even more expensive home for renovation that should bring a seven-figure price when completed next year. I am very proud of their ongoing accomplishments as they grow their business.

My mom's parents were both from northern Maine and of French-Canadian stock. To this day I jokingly call my Dubois and Michaud blood my stubborn half. Because my mom Lillian had turbulent marriages while we were kids, my grandparents' home became our refuge. I will forever be grateful to Nana and Papé for giving me a safe port in which to weather Lillian's storms.

When Chrissy was pregnant with our first grandchild, Locklyn, we were ecstatic. I always teased my children that they may not be ready for kids, but we were! I wanted Rosann and I to be the next generation of Nana and Papé. However, Ryan's stepmom, Denise, already had grandchildren and was called "Nana." Rosann could not have the same moniker.

Being Italian, Rosann decided she wanted the grandkids to call her *Nonna*, Italian for "the one who helps with the children and binds the family together." Call her our matriarch, the name and its meaning fit her to a tee!

Chrissy gave birth at the hospital on January 15, 2014. She wanted her mom to be the first one to see the baby. We were a few minutes late getting to the maternity ward. Ryan's parents were already there, and his mom was quite upset that she was not allowed to see the baby when she arrived. Oh well. You cannot please everyone, but these are not the kind of things to get upset about. It's supposed to be about the baby, not us.

I cannot begin to tell you how special Locklyn is to both of us. Her parents got sick when she was only two weeks old. I was just driving home from the airport after a long, all-night trip. Rosann called and asked me to stop by Chrissy's and pick up the baby. They were worried they would get her sick. So, I picked up Locklyn and we kept her for a few days until Ryan and Chrissy were feeling better. Locklyn is eleven years old now, and she has spent a night per week at our house ever since, except when she's with her father. Our home is her second home. She even drew a picture once of a large house with four adults in it. She wanted all of us to live under one roof. So sweet—you cannot make this stuff up.

As a toddler, Locklyn would "dance" by bouncing on her diapered bottom whenever music was played. As she grew, there was nothing from my dinner plate I couldn't give her that she wouldn't accept.

On winter mornings, I would make myself a cup of coffee and warm up a bottle of formula for Locklyn, then I would wrap her up in a warm blanket and take her and our two golden retrievers outside. I would sit in an Adirondack chair in the backyard while the dogs roamed around. Sipping coffee, Locklyn drank her bottle while she watched the dogs with lazy interest. We bonded early and completely.

When she had trouble sleeping, I would place a hand on her belly and whisper soft nothings until she drifted off to sleep. I remember having our dear friends BJ and Charlotte over for Thanksgiving when Locklyn was just one or two years old. After watching us that day,

Charlotte later told BJ, "I didn't know Rich could be so gentle." I rather liked that observation . . . I think.

Almost two years after Locklyn was born, Chrissy gave birth to Brandt. He was born on November 11, 2016, the day after my birthday. I remember teasing Chrissy with, "Couldn't you have walked around some more the day before?"

We were a little worried at first if we would be able to establish the same kind of relationship with Brandt as we had with Locklyn, because now the attention had to be shared. We should not have worried. We did not keep Brandt overnight until he was a couple of months old, but he made our home his own the same way Locklyn did.

As grandparents, we have been about as involved as anyone could be in their day-to-day lives. We love them so much that it's scary to imagine anything bad happening to them. I told my adult children that I love them very much, but I do not love them like I love these grandchildren, so just get over it. A mother bear has nothing on Rosann or me.

Part of what makes being Nonna and Papé so fun is watching the kids grow up. When they were young, each week brought some new skills or learned vocabulary. I can see why someone would be fascinated by the child-development career field.

The other truly fun thing is observing just how different these two children are in personality, even though they are very obviously siblings in physical characteristics. Locklyn is very much a "girly girl," as they say. She loves stuffed animals and cooking. She speaks softly and cries easily. She is always hesitant with new physical activities such as learning to master some contraption in a kid's playground or riding a bike.

Brandt, on the other hand, is all boy. He can be loud, frenetic in his activities, rushing around hell-bent-for-leather, to the point of ignoring you or even his own safety. He needs to be watched like a hawk! He also likes to tease his sister as he laughs a devilish cackle. That is until the claws come out. Then he had better run!

Lately he has taken a serious interest in airplanes. So much so that

I set him up with a flight simulator and a small piston airplane. I have taken him in a private jet before, and he bugs his mother about flying versus driving to our vacation locations. I hope I am planting a seed that will grow.

Diana's two little girls could not be more different than their cousins. They are smart as a whip and stubborn at the same time. It is amazing to watch them fantasy play and create whole scenarios. You have to watch Josie, because when she wants to go outside, she just heads for the door. I have to keep the doors locked and watch her carefully.

Charlie is so intelligent. For a three-year-old her speech is clear and beyond her years. She is a thinker, reasoning things out. What really pleases us, though, is that Brandt and Locklyn love playing with their cousins. I am hoping this closeness will last a lifetime.

CHAPTER 29

The Frozen Continent

Antarctica, the frozen continent. Fourteen million square kilometers. You can fit the US and Mexico within its dimensions, and Russia is the only country bigger at seventeen million square kilometers. Ice and snowfields can be as deep as five kilometers, with two kilometers being the average depth. There's evidence of a swampy rainforest near Pine Island Glacier from ninety million years ago, yet the temperature extremes today range from -90 to 15 degrees Celsius, depending on season and location.

Twelve million penguins represent eighteen species. Six different species of seals. Eight species of whales, including orcas. Thirty-five species of seabirds. The human population in the winter months is about a thousand researchers and staff. The summer population is about ten thousand, including tourists and crews on cruise ships.

My group of six friends spent ten days on the *Ushuaia*, a 278-foot former NOAA research vessel, along with seventy-eight other passengers and three dozen crew. Alan "Reflux" Cockrell (because he did that a lot during the Drake Passage) had the distinction of traveling to Antarctica with a US scientific expedition when he was just nineteen and in college. He even visited the south pole. After fifty-something years he wanted to plan his encore performance. Of course, this isn't something you do alone, so he talked five of us into joining him: myself, Richard "Limo" Hess (because I ride in limos a lot), Dr. Dennis "Moose" Utley (because he loves to hunt moose), Greg "Click" Tackett (our photography expert), Brian "Cowbell" Sabourin (Mississippi State graduate), and Tom "Bullseye" Kahlert (a dual-rated US Army master aviator and weapons-systems contractor).

Three pilots, two engineers, and a doctor. Between the six of us we brought over two hundred years of experience in everything from aircraft to medicine to weapons systems, but we were not prepared for the stomach-churning challenges and amazing experiences of a ten-day adventure to the 65th parallel south. This was life on a heaving ship, with delightful animal encounters, awesome ice-covered vistas, and one hundred wonderful people from all over the globe.

I doubt any of us will ever go back to Antarctica. It is simply too expensive and physically challenging. However, by putting our memories to paper with a Shutterfly book, we strove to preserve this unique experience for the rest of our lives.

Tom was late to join the group after another friend's new job precluded his going on the trip. He was very excited to accept our invitation, and this preserved our two-to-a-room reservation. Pairs would be Greg and Brian; Alan and Dennis; Tom and I.

The original trip was scheduled for March 2022, the end of the summer season, but due to Argentina's strict COVID lockdown, the trip was rescheduled for January 2023. This was to our advantage as January would be the middle of the southern summer, with better weather, hopefully. A bit of a reprieve, this allowed us more time to prepare. We all started doing research as to the ship's services, predicted weather, clothing requirements, and general expectations.

As it turned out, most of us overpacked, but for good reasons. Our trip would span a large range of climates and temperatures. We planned to meet in Buenos Aires, where it would be in the high eighties, and spend the night before flying to Ushuaia the next day.

Ushuaia was a three-and-a-half-hour flight farther south and claimed to be the most southerly city in the world with summertime highs averaging in the mid-fifties.

The Drake Passage and Antarctica itself were the destinations we needed to pay the most attention to. I found a website that displayed weather and ocean conditions for the passage. The temperature looked consistent, averaging in the forties, but the ocean conditions were concerning. Five-to-eight-meter waves rolling in on a ten-second cycle and winds between twenty-five and fifty-six miles per hour. Even at the height of the summer, the Drake Passage was going to be a challenge for the most intrepid of mariners.

Our itinerary involved planned excursions on the Antarctic Peninsula and the South Shetland Islands. The sheltered waters were expected to be calm with daily temperatures anywhere between three and thirty-two degrees. The skies were mostly cloudy for our trip, and we did have days of significant snowfall and reduced visibility.

All the above meant we needed to be thorough in our clothing selections. For Antarctica itself we would need thermal underwear, wool socks, waterproof gloves, tall waterproof boots, insulated pants, heavy sweaters, a parka with a hood, and a wool cap or balaclava. Living in Alabama and Georgia, we occasionally get significant cold snaps, but they do not last. Living on a mountain in Washington state and hunting in Alaska, Dennis was probably the one most familiar with the expected weather, although I am sure Alan remembered the biting cold and unexpected weather changes from his time at McMurdo Station half a century ago. So, we put our heads together, did our research, and we each bought a lot of winter clothing we might never use again!

Then we made travel arrangements. Four of us planned to meet in Atlanta and fly Delta to Buenos Aires. Alan and Dennis met at DFW in Dallas and flew American. If the airlines were on time, we would all arrive at the EZE airport in Buenos Aires within thirty minutes of each other.

The final piece of the puzzle was getting us all rooms at a good hotel in both Buenos Aires and Ushuaia. Five of us booked the Hilton, but since he came on board so late, Tom had to book another beautiful hotel just a block away. The hotel in Ushuaia was another story, but more on that later.

We had done all we could to prepare for this trip. Everyone was looking forward to a once-in-a-lifetime adventure. Now all we had to do was wait for our departure on January 5.

All six of us arrived in Buenos Aires around nine in the morning, cleared customs and immigration, collected our checked baggage, and went to a meeting point specified by our driver David Boccazzi. He needed two vehicles to carry the six of us plus our baggage to the downtown hotels. We were impressed with how busy both hotels were. After all, this was the summer tourist season and the first year Argentina had lifted its severe COVID restrictions.

Later that afternoon we all got together and found an elegant steak restaurant along the Dique waterway that our hotel recommended. La Cabaña served steaks that most of us felt were quite expensive for just being "okay." After eating, we returned to our hotel rooms for a well-deserved night's sleep since the previous night had been spent upright in an airliner. Tomorrow would be a three-and-a-half-hour flight south to Tierra del Fuego Province (The Land of Fire) and Ushuaia, the southernmost city in the world.

The group caught two different flights on Aerolíneas Argentinas. Making reservations had proved to be a real challenge. Going through a third party, we were the lowest priority, and the airline kept changing our return flight on the eighteenth to a much later time. I finally canceled that reservation and made a direct reservation with the airline.

Ushuaia is a quaint city, surrounded by mountains to the north and the channel to the ocean to the south. It is not as refined as Buenos Aires; rather, it is a small working city, depending greatly on the thousands of tourists that visit during the warmer months.

The Antártida Hotel was a cheap two-star hotel we decided to stay at the night before boarding the ship. We found the check-in process tedious, and with no elevator, we each had to drag our oversized luggage up to the second and third floors.

We went out to look over the town, but that didn't take long. The streets were very crowded with fellow passengers waiting to board a half dozen cruise ships the next day. We bought some souvenirs then found a small out-of-the-way bar to knock back a couple of beers. Dinner was at Chicho's, a local mom-and-pop restaurant that served wonderful food, especially hake, a local fish. The food was so good and the price so reasonable that we went back for lunch the next day before heading to the harbor for boarding.

We were not due on the dock until three in the afternoon for a four o'clock boarding. That morning would be spent double-checking our equipment and communicating with loved ones one last time before setting off on our adventure.

When the *Ushuaia* started down the Beagle Canal the afternoon of our departure, it had to travel about sixty nautical miles to reach the ocean. We had dinner on board, our first of many well-executed meals, riding on calm and steady waters. Everyone went to bed that night not knowing what was in store for us the next morning.

We spent four days total in the Drake Passage, two each way. The trip southbound was bad enough, but the trip northbound was even worse. Heading south we saw five-meter waves, steady thirty-miles-an-hour winds, and five degrees of pitch with a solid twenty-five degrees of rolling motion. For the return, the weather was even more severe, with winds peaking around fifty miles per hour and eight-meter waves! The boat pitched ten degrees up and down and rolled what seemed like forty-five degrees. You could feel and hear the propellers cavitate as they rose out of the water. Then they'd bite down again as the stern lowered in the swell.

Dishes, silverware, and glasses were sent crashing at times during meals. How the waitstaff served anything under these conditions is a testament to their skill and perseverance! You could tell how many passengers were seasick by the number of empty chairs at any given meal. At times it seemed to be nearly half of them. Everyone had Dramamine or seasick patches to settle their stomachs. Greg and Brian even bought a watch-like device that shot electric jolts into their wrists and the nerves of their hands. The idea was to distract the mind from the stomach and focus on the hands instead. It seemed to work.

The crew reminded us not to go outside during the passage, but if you did, to do so within sight of the bridge in case you're thrown overboard. I was surprised when some passengers went outside at the stern-most door just to get a picture or video of the roiling ocean. I went to the bridge during the crossing back. The spray from the waves covered the bridge windows, and we had to hold on for dear life so as not to be thrown to the floor!

In the common lounge area, I watched people get thrown off-balance by the ship's extreme motion and stumble headfirst into the wall. How we didn't end up with severe injuries is a miracle because half the passengers were older retirees. In fact, on a recent cruise, a passenger tried to take a shower during the passage and was thrown to the floor, breaking ribs and puncturing a lung on the raised metal lip. The captain had no choice but to complete the two-day crossing, turn around, and head straight back to Argentina. Even Alan was thrown off his upper bunk while trying to climb down, slamming his face into the desk and breaking it in the process. Thank goodness for sheltered waters when we reached Antarctica.

Overall, it was a fantastic trip. For more than forty years I have traveled the world, first for Uncle Sam and then for Delta Air Lines. From Moscow to Johannesburg, Seattle to Santiago, Beijing to Sydney, I have seen it all . . . except Antarctica. I have traveled throughout the Arctic, yet Antarctica was different, like visiting an alien planet. Every minute there was another stunning vista to be captured, if only I could frame it properly in the viewfinder.

I was disappointed not to see any orcas, but I am sure the penguins and seals didn't mind. There were so many penguins that your mind was numbed by their numbers, losing the sense of wonder, although I never tired of the stark and beautiful scenery.

The boat's crew did an admirable job adjusting our schedule due to the ever-changing weather. I particularly appreciated the kitchen staff, who served great food under some of the harshest conditions.

Sometimes on the excursions I just stood still, soaked in the clean, crisp air, and marveled at the never-ending, unspoiled mountains and glaciers. At moments like that I felt small, realizing just how little I am in this vast wilderness. It also made me appreciate the blessings I have been given: my health, family, and friends, especially the new ones I made on this trip.

Half the ship's company were retirement age, and this was not an easy trip for some. The extreme pitching and rolling of the ship made for very challenging conditions. Only .5 percent of the world's population has ever traveled to Antarctica. I will never go back again, but I am so glad I did it once, and I will treasure the memories for the rest of my life.

CHAPTER 30

Author, Author

I have been writing for my entire adult life. During my twenty-eight years in the military, I wrote countless performance reports for both myself and those under my command. I got good enough at it that others would come to me for help writing theirs. You wanted to address several critical points: primary duty performance, attitude, relative standing among your peers, and future potential, with special emphasis on an officer's ability to assume greater levels of responsibility.

During the twelve years I served in the Mississippi Air National Guard, I wrote numerous leadership articles for the statewide national guard magazine, which was distributed to both army and air force units. I was once told I needed to consider my audience and dumb it down a bit, that my articles read too much like a college course . . . hmm.

I started flying warbirds in 2001 and before long I was writing all sorts of articles about flying safety, aircraft maintenance, formation responsibilities and procedures, travel logs about my thirteen deliveries to overseas customers, training, leadership, and many other subjects. I was published dozens of times in half a dozen US publications as well as aviation magazines in South Africa, Brazil, and Italy.

I enjoyed writing more than I realized, but I wanted to do more. I started writing this memoir twenty years ago, then put it down when I bought the aircraft maintenance company in 2007. I always intended to finish it, but I felt I was too busy over the last seventeen years to give it the attention it deserved. I also felt the intervening two decades added enough experience and perspective that I finally had something worthwhile to add to the story.

In the meantime, an opportunity came about that I was not expecting. My former squadron mate, fellow warbird pilot, and overall good friend, Alan Cockrell, had a long-term friend who died a few years ago. He had also been an air force and airline pilot. He had started to write a military thriller about a conflict between the US and Russia. His brother asked Alan if he wanted to take on the task of finishing the rough draft and preparing it for publication. Alan called me and asked if I wanted to be a part of this challenging endeavor.

I say challenging because the draft was eleven hundred pages long, dated, and in serious need of not just editing but also updating. Alan and I slaved for the best part of four years to make *Night of the Bear* what it is today. Our arguments about what to cut, what to leave in, and what updates or changes to make could be quite spirited at times. Alan is the better writer since he has already published several books. He is great at seeing the forest from the trees. I was better at seeing the trees.

When it was all said and done after a solid ten editing passes, we had whittled it down to 420 pages with little fluff. The characters and political landscape were brought up to the present, and the novel was a hit with our beta readers. We received many comments about how they could not put the book down. Buoyed by the feedback, we worked tirelessly to entice an agent or publisher. If needed, we would have self-published. This book simply ended up being too good to take no for an answer.

We also had some great ideas about a storyline for a sequel involving China and the US. Alan graciously handed the writing responsibility to me, and he provided editing. I completed the first draft of *Red Tide* in December 2024, five months after first bringing pen to paper. I have my fingers crossed that it will be as well received as *Night of the Bear*.

This work is not for everyone, but it has been tremendously

educational learning how to write a novel. I never would have thought about all the dos and don'ts. We were ultimately successful and signed a contract with Koehler Books in early 2024, and I cannot wait to see this labor of love in print. Thank you, Alan, for all your patience with me as I learned what it takes to write a book.

To follow up on this success, as I write this paragraph in the fall of 2024, I will have officially finished writing my memoir. It has only been in the making for the last twenty years! I can't say enough how proud and excited I am that Koehler will be publishing it as well. Now, let's see how many people want to read it!

CHAPTER 31

Final Thoughts and Wisdom Gained

I turned seventy-one years old this November. I think it is normal to look back on your life in later years and reflect on how you have spent it. I have done that throughout my adult life, but age brings a certain wisdom that you do not possess when you are younger. Of course, there are regrets. There are too many times that I wish I could do or say something differently, or even just do or say something in the first place.

Ego, ignorance, and selfish behavior are embedded in each of us. I have certainly met some truly wonderful people, but none of us are perfect. We all make mistakes. In fact, I believe most people are emotional cowards. They would rather turn their back on someone or some situation than face the moment and find a solution. It is easier to walk away than to accept responsibility for a bad situation. On top of that, self-awareness is a challenge for everyone. I will ask again: How many of us are brave enough to look in the mirror and see what is truly there? I still struggle every day with seeing myself in an honest way. Rosann must have the patience of Job because she is still helping me to find the kinder, gentler me.

I also see people who compromise their beliefs regularly for the sake of selfish gain. How often do you thoroughly consider your beliefs, and make a commitment to follow them every day? Or do you break your own rules for the sake of a short-term pleasure, a financial gain, or an advantage over someone else?

I think about such things daily, because as flawed as I am, I am always trying to be better than the day before. One day at a time. One victory at a time. It can be very difficult to stand by your convictions when they mark you as an outsider, but the integrity it takes to do so is important to leading a fulfilling life.

We grew up with considerably less than what our children and grandchildren have today. We did without many things. Clothes, furniture, and even cars were hand-me-downs. We did not need, nor could we afford, the next greatest thing, whatever that may be. Yes, life could be tough, but we turned out okay. An army friend used to say, "That which does not kill you makes you stronger." I agree.

I remember when I was first hired at Delta. My first-year salary was $21,600, half of what I was making as an air force captain. Our three children were young, so Rosann needed to be a stay-at-home mom for a while. The additional money earned in the national guard made up for the shortfall, otherwise we would have been much worse off.

I was activated for ten months for the first Desert Storm in 1990, only three years after being hired by Delta. Near the end of my activation, Rebecca Chase from ABC News came to the house and interviewed the family while I was back in the US running a staging operation. Their story's emphasis was on the financial impact of being activated. I told her you had to live a little below your means in preparation for such an event. Later in my life, as a senior wide-body captain and while running my own business, I had much fewer worries about money, but the lessons of my youth, and again in the beginning at Delta, helped me develop a good financial discipline that I have used my entire life.

I would say I have a typical type A personality. I am intelligent, hardworking, and give my all to whatever I decide to pursue. And I expect everyone else to do the same.

Well, it doesn't always work that way. Some people are smart, some are talented, some are both. Some have a desire to lead others, some only want to do their job and be left alone. Not everyone can take a group and lead them through an important endeavor. However, as an officer in the air force, we were all expected to grow into leadership positions. In fact, that was an important item in our fitness reports. Airplane crews, squadron enlisted members, and additional duties gave each of us an opportunity to develop our leadership skills. These are the kinds of skills often sought by civilian companies, and I found them very helpful as I built up five companies over the last twenty years.

Part of my personality has been my never-ending belief that I can change others when there is a conflict or a troubling situation. It took me fifty years to finally realize I only have a limited ability to change other people. People can be stubborn. Once they decide what they believe about someone or something, getting them to change their mind involves getting them to see where they are wrong. Remember what I said about looking in the mirror. Admitting guilt or to being wrong is as difficult as being self-aware.

So, what to do? I often find myself praying for guidance, and for others to see His light in me. But instead of changing the other person, it is usually me that changes to accommodate the situation. I find that fascinating, because it means He really does listen to my prayers. I don't ask for *things*. Instead, I ask for the strength and patience to deal with the situation.

I also pray every day for the health and safety of my children and grandchildren. I am sure Chrissy and Diana are tired of me always pointing out the dangers of this or that, but I know my heart would be broken forever if anything ever happened to one of my grandkids. As I have said, I tease my children that I love them, but I do not love them like I love those grandkids.

I look at how our society has changed over the decades. Is Generation Z the latest group? I don't know anymore. Regardless, they make me shake my head in wonder. All of my generation were raised by parents and grandparents who lived through the Great Depression, World War II, and the Korean War. We were expected to do our chores, and to respect our elders, police, teachers, and anyone else in a position of authority. That is not how it is today. Teenagers and adults bring weapons into schools, office buildings, bars, and concerts, inflicting as much tragedy as possible. The number of massacres these last few decades is staggering.

Growing up, we were taught that you start at the bottom, and you pay your dues, earning your promotions as your skill sets increase. I remember being told early in my air force career to treat my current job like it is the best job in the world, and doors of opportunity would open for me. Now young people expect to receive a high salary right out of school, with their continued education paid for by their employer. I paid for almost all my higher education and advanced flying licenses and ratings with the help of the GI Bill. No one gave me anything. I either earned it by my efforts or paid for it out of my own pocket. If you want to feel accomplished, then work for the achievement and the success will be that much sweeter.

I remember being home in New York for Christmas and New Year's when I was still on active duty. Rosann's sister Marie and her husband Doug invited us to a New Year's Eve party. I sat for a while talking to a schoolteacher and an accountant. Somehow, we got on the subject of money, and how much each of them had saved to date. This was around 1980, and the figure being bandied about was ten thousand.

Well, I did not have ten thousand dollars yet saved. I think I had half that amount. I spoke up and said, "If the only thing you take home twice a month is your paycheck, then you are missing something very important." The accountant looked at me with confusion on his face while the schoolteacher just nodded his head in agreement.

I sometimes wonder how many people live their adult lives doing the kind of work they truly love. I suspect it is the vast minority. My two oldest children found what they wanted to do while they were still in college, with a little push from Rosann and me since we knew them pretty darn well. Diana, on the other hand, took into her mid-thirties before she found her niche flipping houses.

Part of why finding what you are good at, or like doing, is so important is because we give our best effort to activities in which we see success. No one likes to lose or do poorly. It's no fun, and it demotivates you. On many occasions I have reminded my children to work hard, become as expert as possible in their chosen field, and be the person other people turn to when a problem exists. In other words, be the person others know they can depend on.

I have learned many other lessons that I have tried to impart to my children. Do not waste other people's time. Always be honest, for the sake of your integrity. Treat other people's money as you would your own. Always return communication. Give compliments in public, give criticism in private. And never let your boss hear bad news from above his or her head. Make sure they hear it from you first. These are all lessons I have learned through the years and applied to every endeavor, whether it was personal or business.

At the beginning of this book, I asked myself, "How did things get so bad?" The truthful answer is that they are not bad at all! Sure, I have made many mistakes. I have been used or even abused by different people through the years. I will be the first to admit that these actions hurt me, and sometimes they made me doubt myself. However, I eventually realized that my faith in Him carried me through those difficult times. Remember what I said earlier: I pray a lot, but often my prayers lead to changes within myself, rather than changes within my circumstances.

My mother's abandonment turned my focus more fully on my own growing family. In the summer of 2024, twenty of Rosann's and my family spent a week in a beautiful two-hundred-year-old villa in Tuscany, Italy. The previous summer we had twenty-four of us in a ten-bedroom house in the north Georgia mountains.

None of my brothers will have anything to do with me even though I have reached out. Two of them seem to be following my mother's wishes of cutting me off forever. Since she left her meager estate to them and nothing to me, I'd imagine it's easier to just pretend I don't exist. My brother Jeff in Connecticut is polite but does not seem to want to make any effort. I think I simply came along too late in his life to establish a good relationship, and once our father died, the connection was broken.

The good news is that I get along very well with my sister Ann and cousin Patty, who also live in Connecticut. In fact, Patty and one of her girlfriends joined us in Italy. Patty's husband, Conan, stayed home for the week to care for their autistic son, James. I greatly admire his dedication to his two sons.

I love Ann. She is a crazy dog lover and has been involved with rescues for many years. It concerns me though when you walk in her front door and you are greeted by half a dozen canines, most of which are mastiffs, pit bulls, or some combination of either. As long as they don't eat me!

Something I have found interesting within my world of aviation—and perhaps it is partially because we spend so much time away from home—is that your friends and fellow aviators become your family. Especially as I've aged, I've found that my older fellow pilots, especially those with military backgrounds, are the people with whom I share the most similar worldview.

Life can fill you up or suck you dry. It is up to you how you choose to deal with it. And while I'm proud of all the adventures and challenges I've experienced over the last fifty years, I'm trying to make family my highest priority. At the end of the day, you have to decide what you want written on your gravestone. *He was never home. We didn't really know her. He loved money more than us.* Probably not what you envision.

I have lived a truly blessed life, and I am still enjoying new experiences every year. There is no continent I have not traveled to, including Antarctica. I have friends from dozens of countries all over the world. I am considered an expert in my field. And I feel as if I have achieved Maslow's highest level: self-actualization. But of even more importance, I feel loved by my children, grandchildren, sister, cousin, and even Rosann's family. What more can I ask for?

My last thought: What good is success if you do not find ways to pass along your knowledge to others? I consult Diana on business topics all the time. Rosann counts on me to handle various aspects of our lives. My copilots who go on to airline careers or get checked out as newly minted captains come back and thank me for preparing them for that "next big step." These are the things that truly make me feel good about myself and the life I have lived. It is important that we have a purpose in life and actively pursue that purpose. Well, I have multiple purposes.

I will end with a single line we used to say in the military: Lead, follow, or get out of the way! You are only on this earth for a short amount of time. Go live your life!

ACKNOWLEDGMENTS

It took me more than fifteen years to write *High Flight: A Pilot's Journey Through Life*. I didn't want to just write a book. I wanted to write something that would be worthy of others giving their time to read it. I wanted to do more than just describe the adventures, trials, tribulations, failures, and successes of my life. Indeed, there have been many of each. I wanted to impart what I had learned from each of my experiences. I believe that what you do with the wisdom gained is more important than the experience that gave you that wisdom. I have truly tried.

I want to thank everyone at Koehler Books for believing in what I was trying so hard to accomplish here. John Koehler was enthusiastic from day one. Danielle Koehler is smart, artistic, and always has answers for my never-ending questions. Hannah Tonsor Burke has been my editor on two books now. I admire her spunk and her patience as she has guided me through the maze of book writing and the proper use of the English language. Thank you all.

Last, but not least, I want to offer my special thanks to Alan Cockrell: squadron mate, editor, mentor, fellow warbird pilot and adventurer, and friend. Alan encouraged me, pushed me, cajoled me, teased me, and taught me to be the writer I am today. I have expanded my business opportunities and writing skills under his careful guidance. Life is infinitely more lived because of him. I am forever in his debt.

www.ingramcontent.com/pod-product-compliance
Lightning Source LLC
LaVergne TN
LVHW041918070526
838199LV00051BA/2656